"Why do some get stuck and others bounce? I started reading with the intention of discovering the answer and wound up seeing myself in these pages. Liberating! Life-giving! Your desire to help someone else discover joy may be a gift to your own heart."

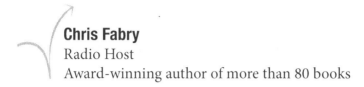

Chris Fabry
Radio Host
Award-winning author of more than 80 books

"*Building Bounce* brings that essential transparency to know you are reading reality. Marcus and Stefanie tell stories together that combine the great truths we usually cannot apply in ways that just fit and make sense. Reading this book will be nearly useless but *practicing* this book is going to change your life and relationships. I want everyone I know to be *Building Bounce*!"

Jim Wilder
Author | Neurotheologian
Life Model Works

"There are many things we like about *Building Bounce*! One is the clarity. Marcus and Stefanie wrote a remarkably clear book that puts words to essentials we need in order to develop emotional resilience to be our best selves. Second, this book is compelling! Once you pick it up, you will not want to put it down. Putting the *Bounce* principles into practice changes you, your character, your relationships and your life. Much like baking a cake, growing emotional resilience requires specific ingredients for success. When done right, the results are magnificent! Read *Building Bounce*. Give copies to your friends. Our world needs this!"

Chris & Jen Coursey
Authors | Speakers
THRIVEtoday

D1547402

"Marcus and Stefanie have done an excellent job blending complex topics like attachment theory, brain science, and biblical principles to create a simple approach to building resilience. Regardless of your current ability to bounce back from difficult situations, you will likely find the information and exercises throughout the book practical and simple to use. I'm excited to have this book as a resource both personally and professionally!"

Melissa Finger, MS
Executive Director | Counselor
Seek First Ministries

"There is a new and better psychology grounded in neuroscience break-throughs that is displacing much of the past guesswork in this fascinating and noble field of study. Oddly, much of what the research has unveiled confirms the ancient wisdom of the Bible. It's easy to see in retrospect. In *Building Bounce*, Warner and Hinman reveal how this better psychology relates to and integrates with the outstanding biblical value and virtue of relational-joy-based resilient endurance. They provide practical explanations, examples, illustrations and practices that make such transformation concrete and authentic. Read this game-changing book!"

Pastor Michael Sullivant
CEO
Life Model Works

"In the course of life, some people's life pursuit causes them to achieve some-thing called 'convergence.' It is when a lifetime of study, skills, relational ca-pacity, inquiry, and wisdom converge into a distilled sense of vision that not only guides that person's life, but also gives them the ability to convey truth to others that can be readily assimilated. In *Building Bounce*, Marcus, aided (and perhaps catalyzed by) Stefanie, demonstrates convergence, and offers it bountifully to others. I have read Marcus' other books as well. This one is his best so far, beautifully conveying his heart for ministry and relationships. Stefanie brings her treasure trove of skills working with some of the world's most wounded. Together, they offer to every reader the opportunity to have a better and more fulfilling life in every dimension. I cannot overstate the profundity that this superbly written and wonderfully organized book offers to absolutely every reader."

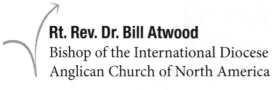

Rt. Rev. Dr. Bill Atwood
Bishop of the International Diocese
Anglican Church of North America

BUILDING BOUNCE

how to grow emotional resilience

MARCUS WARNER | STEFANIE HINMAN

Published by Deeper Walk International.

First Edition May, 2020 / Printed in the United States of America

ISBN: 978-1-7327510-4-0

Deeper Walk International
13295 Illinois St. #223
Carmel, IN 46032

www.DeeperWalkInternational.org

BUILDING BOUNCE

how to grow emotional resilience

MARCUSWARNER | **STEFANIE**HINMAN

DEEPER
WALK

author books

MARCUS WARNER

The 4 Habits of Joy-Filled Marriages with Chris M. Coursey

The Solution of Choice with Jim Wilder

Slaying the Monster

Rare Leadership with Jim Wilder

Understanding the Wounded Heart

The Spirit-Filled Home

What Every Believer Should Know About Spiritual Warfare

A Deeper Walk Guide to Advent

How to Grow Joy

REAL Prayer

3-2-1 Bible Study Method

D.I.D. Primer

Toward a Deeper Walk

The Deeper Walk Guide to the Bible

STEFANIE HINMAN

The Amazing Marvelous Milly

TABLE OF CONTENTS

author notes

STEFANIE

In my first five years out of college, I worked at a residential home for children with severe behavioral disorders and a local hospice. The children I worked with had seen more adversity, trauma, and loss in their few short years than most people experience in a life time.

I often found myself wondering if our best practices of care were really helping. I could work for hours with a child on emotional expressiveness or learning to feel safe. However, if the family system or community culture wasn't emotionally safe, the child would be punished for expressing their emotions or worse re-traumatized by the adults in their lives who were stuck in old dysfunctional patterns of relating. I learned that children can only heal and grow in family systems and community cultures that give them the physical, emotional, and spiritual nutrients they need to heal and grow.

Even though I often felt discouraged in those early years, there was one crucial question that emerged. This one question still drives me as a mom and a therapist…

"Why do some kids bounce back after trauma and some get stuck in it?"

Child after child, family after family, patterns began to emerge. There were certain key factors that created strong healthy families, and strong healthy families create strong healthy kids.

I was then asked to help create a resilience building program for children. Up until this point there had been research on what makes adults resilient but very little on children.

This question became the focus of my work. But it was motherhood that became the most motivating factor in my search for finding how to equip children to thrive in a world filled with adversity. After years of research, study, and practice, I learned a few things that I consider very good news…

1) No matter how old you are, you can learn to become more resilient.

2) The more resilient you are, the more resilient the children who depend on you will become.

MARCUS

Building Bounce® is about growing your ability to bounce back from hard experiences. Some call this resilience. Others call it hardiness or grit. The idea is not to prevent feeling pain or negative emotions. Nor is the idea that you should be happy all the time. Building bounce is learning how to grow both your capacity to handle stress and your skills in bouncing back from it.

A few years ago, I learned about Stefanie Hinman's curriculum for helping children build emotional resilience. It was packed with practical tools and teaching. I was impressed, and we discussed writing a parent resource together. After much discussion, however, we decided to write this book because it isn't just children who need to learn how to build bounce. We live in a world that seems to be increasing in adversity and decreasing in joy. All of us could benefit from extra bounce.

Our goal in writing this book is to explain the theory behind growing resilience and to provide practical tools you can use both in a variety of settings such as growing your own emotional capacity, parenting your children in ways that build joy, and helping others who live low-joy lives learn the skills that grow joy.

We call this the ABCs of Building Bounce because we have reduced the essential practices for growing resilience to A-B-C.

- » Appreciation
- » Beliefs
- » Connections

People who bounce back quickly from upset emotions practice appreciation regularly, take their thoughts captive and foster healthy beliefs, and develop strong connections with God and others. In this book, we hope to walk you through the theory and practice that will help you live with greater bounce!

> Reader Note: For clarity we've generally marked "I" statements throughout the text with the narrating author's name. However, if you read "I" or "me" in the text and it is not clearly attributed to an author, it is likely Marcus writing.

CHAPTER ONE
the secret to emotional resilience

Life is hard. We all get overwhelmed at times. But some people seem to be able to handle hardship better than others. They bounce back from their upset emotions faster than most. It may even seem like some people are just born happy. But is this true? Is there a secret to the emotional resilience that gets people through life? If so, don't you want to know what it is?

Thanks to the latest brain science,[1] we now understand that there is a secret to emotional resilience. It can be summed up in one word—joy. The more joy you have, the more hardship you can handle. High-joy people bounce back from the hardships of life faster than low-joy people. The more normal it becomes to feel joy, the easier it is to handle upsetting emotions. The faster you return to joy after getting upset, the easier it is to feel like yourself.

Joy is often seen as the "icing on the cake" of life. It's a nice surprise when it happens, but we don't think of it as foundational to life. However, joy is like the air in the ball that makes it bounce. If you don't have enough joy, the ball doesn't bounce back properly. It can even go flat.

Many adults struggle with depression, anxiety, and other emotions that drag them down and can feel overwhelming. These emotions will take over one's life, so people who struggle in this way tend to be highly motivated to find a solution. For most of my life, I (Marcus) described myself

---

1 | Most of the brain science research in this book is based on the writings of such authors as Jim Wilder, Allan Schore, Daniel Siegel, and Daniel Amen.

as "slightly depressed." A few years ago, I had a series of panic attacks that took me off guard and started a year-long battle with anxiety that left me very motivated to figure out how to "bounce back" from both low-level depression and high-level anxiety.

It has helped me to think of my capacity for joy as a container capable of growing. It grows bigger every time it hits its joy limit. To grow this container, three essential tasks need to be done: 1) Repair, 2) Relational Joy, 3) Rest.

Repair relates to emotional healing and spiritual warfare. It involves taking thoughts captive and healing memories that fuel negative thinking. This type of repair can be thought of as patching the leaks in your joy container. *Building Bounce* will not be addressing issues of repair. We recommend *Understanding the Wounded Heart* and *What Every Believer Should Know About Spiritual Warfare* for guidance on repairing the holes in your joy container.

Relational joy means becoming more intentional about time with people, especially family, and also time with God—especially time spent in appreciation.

Rest represents margin. It is impossible to grow joy if you have no Sabbath and no sleep. Exhausting yourself and then crashing is not the same as resting. Rest requires a healthy routine.

We wrote *Building Bounce* to give you a simple process for building a rhythm of relational joy and rest and for helping others build theirs. The process for building this rhythm can be remembered as easily as A-B-C.

THE ABCS OF BOUNCE

The ABCs of building bounce are appreciation, beliefs, and connections. People who form strong habits around these three practices will grow emotional resilience. Here is a quick summary of the ABCs.

A – Appreciation. We have combined quieting and appreciation into one step. The practice of appreciation should lead to both joy and peace. Sometimes we need to quiet before we can appreciate, and sometimes appreciation helps us quiet. Appreciation is needed in order to train your brain to focus on what there is to enjoy in life. Staying in a state of appreciation for five minutes or longer two or more times each day is an important habit for growing the joy center in your brain.[2]

The fastest way to jumpstart growing your capacity for joy is to spend five minutes writing out what you appreciate, where you feel that emotion in your body, and then sharing what you appreciate with someone else. Sharing appreciation with others takes it from simply being a task we perform to an experience of relational joy. Doing this twice a day as an ongoing habit will help you grow your capacity to bounce back from hard emotions.[3]

B – Beliefs. Your brain needs to be trained to build a narrative that is anchored in optimism. Optimism can be defined as the belief that God works all things together for good for those who love Him and are called according to His purposes (Romans 8:28). When our brains are anchored in optimism, we see our lives as a story of redemption.

---

2 | We will have more to say about the joy center later. It is the part of your brain that grows with the experience of joy and rest.

3 | A study at Indiana University ("The effects of gratitude expression on neural activity" published by Prathik Kini, Joel Wong, Sydney McInnis, Nicole Gabana, and Joshua Brown) showed that half an hour each day spent writing letters of appreciation significantly improved emotional resilience. **In a personal conversation with Marcus Warner, Dr. Jim Wilder said** he routinely gave his clients the assignment of practicing appreciation for five minutes twice a day for two to three months, which resulted in significant growth in their emotional capacity.

When pessimism reigns, we see our lives as a story of ruin. Too many of us have brains that have been trained to only focus on what there is to fear in life. We have a hard time disconnecting from the negatives long enough to practice appreciation and share joy. To help us build beliefs anchored in optimism, the apostle Paul encouraged us to spend time thinking about whatever is good, true, lovely, excellent, and praiseworthy (Philippians 4:8).

WHEN OUR BRAINS ARE ANCHORED IN OPTIMISM, WE SEE OUR LIVES AS A STORY OF REDEMPTION.

One tool for helping you manage your beliefs is a simple journaling exercise. Ask God to show you what beliefs are driving your upsetting emotions. Write the thoughts that come to your mind. List them—anywhere from one to four thoughts. Then ask Jesus to show you what replacement thoughts He has for you. Write those down and share them with someone else. Exercises like this can help with moderate level emotions. If you are struggling with a deeply entrenched belief system, there is other healing work that will need to be done.

C – Connections. Isolation is a killer when it comes to growing joy. Knowing that you are not alone with your problems and emotions is important to building bounce. Feeling safe, calm, and connected helps you grow your capacity to deal with hard things. Knowing you belong to a people gives you the security of knowing others will walk through your hard issues with you. Most of us, however, wait for others to create connection with us. Instead, we want to equip you with skills that can help you create connection wherever you go.

Not only is it important to create connection with people, but it is also important to create a connection with God. A strong connection with God serves as an anchor even in those times when you are cut off from others, and it gives you confidence that, no matter what happens, you are never alone.

For all of these reasons and more, learning the skills to create connection is essential to building bounce. An example of a skill that can help you build connection is being intentional about making people smile. You can't make everyone smile, but, if in the course of the day, you see four people and you can get three of them to smile, you will increase your joy—and theirs! I often do this with baristas at coffee shops, people helping me check out at stores, as well as with people I know. One simple way is to show curiosity about something you notice.

For example, one cashier seemed very preoccupied and hadn't smiled at anyone in line. I (Marcus) made it my goal to get him to smile. I noticed he had tattoos on one arm, and I said, "That's an interesting picture. Is there a story behind that?" He immediately made eye contact and told me how it always made him think of a friend. So, I smiled at him and said, "That's a very honoring thing to do." He smiled, and I smiled too as we finished our business, knowing I had added a little joy to his day.

The goal is to make someone's day a little brighter by spreading joy. This makes them feel seen and valued. Plus, when you share joy with someone else, it increases your joy. It's a win-win.

WHAT IS JOY?

As an experience in the brain, joy is always relational. This surprises some people, because they are often alone when they feel joy. They may also have a lot of relationships that don't produce joy, so the idea that joy is dependent on relationships feels a little scary. However, the part of your brain that experiences joy is located in the non-verbal right hemisphere of the brain. This part of your brain is where most of your relational circuitry is. It is also where you react to situations faster than you can think about them.

You feel joy, sadness, shame, anger, and other emotions involuntarily. They happen before you think about them. This means joy is not a choice. It is a feeling.[4] It is a reaction you have to being happy to be with someone. If you want a good picture of this, ask a grandparent, "When your grandchild sees you and squeals with delight, do you have to choose to feel joy?" You will probably get a laugh. At moments like this, you often start smiling before you even realize you are doing it.

From your brain's perspective, joy can be defined as relational happiness. Joy is the feeling of being happy to be with someone. Joy creates a twinkle in our eyes, a smile on our faces, and floods our bodies with positive energy.

WE NEED A RHYTHM OF JOY AND REST IN ORDER TO LIVE AT OUR BEST.

Not long ago I (Marcus) was in a coffee shop with my adult daughter, when she got a phone call from an old college friend. I still smile when I remember how she reacted. As soon as she saw the name on her screen, it was like someone dropped a joy bomb in the cafe. She simultaneously exploded out of her chair, laughed with delight, caught my eye to excuse herself non-verbally, grabbed her phone, and went outside to talk. Through the window, I could see the twinkle in her eyes and the excitement in her body language as she walked back and forth talking with her friend. That is the power of joy.

---

4 | Rejoicing is a choice. Praise is a choice. Appreciation is a choice. There are many choices you can make that lead to joy, but the experience of joy is an emotion that happens in the relational center of your brain, and we can't simply choose to have that feeling.

The counterpart to joy is peace. Joy is the high-energy feeling of shared excitement. Peace is the low-energy feeling of contentment. It is the feeling of being safe, calm, and connected. Throughout the book, we will often refer to joy as the key to emotional capacity. It should be understood, however, that we always mean the rhythm of joy and rest that includes peace and contentment. For example, joy should always end in rest. If you spend time with friends playing board games and eating nachos (or whatever makes you smile), the joy you feel should lead to a time of quiet later. The high joy followed by the low-level quiet creates a complete experience that grows your capacity for joy.

Is joy a choice?

The idea that joy is a choice has been comforting to many people, so let's take a moment to explore this idea. Joy, as we are defining it, is an experience that takes place in the right hemisphere of the brain. It happens in the right orbital prefrontal cortex as dopamine, oxytocin, and other chemicals flow there. This part of your brain—we call it the joy center—grows as we experience a rhythm of joy and rest. Whereas joy is experienced in the right hemisphere of the brain, choices take place in the left hemisphere of the brain. The flow of activity in the brain moves from right to left. This means that I cannot simply choose to have a feeling. However, this does not mean there are no choices I can make and nothing I can do if I don't feel joy.

What the left side of your brain excels at is problem solving. In this case, the problem it is trying to solve is how to feel more joy. While it can't simply flip a switch and activate that feeling, the problem-solving part of my brain can choose to do things that make joy more likely. Appreciation or praise are great examples. I can choose to rejoice in the Lord by praising Him and practicing appreciation. At first this may be a "sacrifice of praise" because I don't feel the emotions. But eventually, if my relational circuits re-engage and my joy center gets back online, the feelings will come.

When it comes to joy, the primary job of beliefs and choices is to help us get the relational circuits in the right hemisphere of our brain back online. We will have a lot to say about how we do this later in the book.

When people say they are choosing joy, it is more accurate to say they are choosing a different attitude or focusing on a new perspective. Such choices can make joy more likely, but it is not quite the same thing as choosing joy.

Joy and the Brain

Contrary to popular opinion, no one is born happy.[5] As an infant, you have the capacity to experience joy for a moment here or there,[6] but this part of your brain is largely undeveloped at birth. This part of your brain only grows through human interaction. Babies and toddlers who experience lots of relational happiness through engagement with other people will experience tremendous growth in this part of their brain. Babies and toddlers who don't experience relational happiness will enter childhood without fully developing the part of the brain that experiences joy. This underdeveloped capacity for joy can affect them for the rest of their lives if something isn't done to intervene and build that capacity.

5 | There is evidence that some people are born with a genetic predisposition to joy. (See the online article by Kelly Miller at PositivePsychology.com "Is Happiness Genetic and What Causes It?") However, predispositions increase the likelihood of something happening; they are not direct causes. Our point here is that joy is not present at birth. It can't be present, because the part of the brain (the prefrontal cortex) that experiences joy is undeveloped at birth.

6 | E. James Wilder, *The Complete Guide to Living with Men* (Pasadena, CA: Shepherd's House, Inc.) 1993, 1997, 2004. 'At two to three months of age a region of the brain, **which was not developed at birth**, begins to grow. This area, called the right prefrontal cortex, will become the top of the command center in the brain" (p. 16 – bold type added).

Emotional resilience depends on two physical changes in the brain that every child needs to experience. The first change is the development of a large joy center. The technical term for this part of your brain is the right orbital pre-frontal cortex. This part of the brain is unformed at birth and needs to grow or it will have disastrous consequences for a child's ability to bounce back from hardship. This doesn't mean they will have no capacity to deal with stress, but that the lack of development increases the inevitability of attachment issues, addictions, and emotional and relational overwhelm.

The second important brain development is the creation of joy pathways. These are neural pathways that are formed as neurons first link together in a chain and eventually get wrapped in white matter—a process called myelination. As we noted before, these pathways are completely unformed at birth. No child is born with the ability to bounce back from painful emotions. These pathways are formed and grown through practice as adults meet babies, toddlers, and children in their big emotions and help them quiet and recover. Let's take a closer look at these two crucial elements of building bounce.

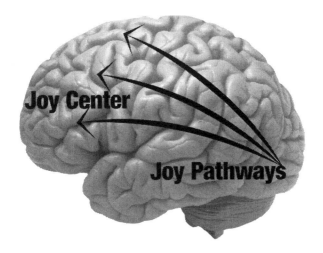

The Joy Center

Infants and toddlers who live in high-joy environments can quickly grow large joy centers in the front right side of their brains. In the best cases, the joy center can grow to fill a quarter to a third of the right side of your brain.[7] Growing a large joy center increases your capacity to feel joy and share it with others. You feel joy more easily and share it more spontaneously when this part of your brain is well-developed.

YOUR BRAIN'S CAPACITY TO EXPERIENCE JOY HAS THE ABILITY TO GROW FOR AS LONG AS YOU LIVE.

In sharp contrast to this, infants and toddlers who live in low-joy environments don't get the relational interaction they need. Consequently, they develop much smaller joy centers and a much lower capacity for joy. A baby who is surrounded by a happy family with lots of people willing to engage with them in both joy and rest will thrive. A baby who is surrounded by angry people, anxious voices, and hopelessness will not only miss out on the good stuff they need in order to grow joy, they will experience trauma from these overwhelming emotions if they are left to deal with them by themselves and not comforted relationally.

The good news is that your brain's capacity to experience joy has the ability to grow for as long as you live. This is one of the main reasons we wrote this book. No matter how large your joy center is now, you can learn skills and habits that can increase its size and, with it, your capacity to live with joy.

---

7 | *The Complete Guide to Living with Men.* 'This area, known as the prefrontal cortex, comes to occupy 35% of the adult brain' (p. 12).

Joy Pathways

Around eighteen months of age, a child's body begins to produce a new set of hormones and chemicals that create some pretty significant changes. For the first time, these little ones can experience extreme emotions. Instead of anger, they can feel rage. Instead of fear, they can feel terror. During this stage of development their brains need help from mom, dad, and others to learn how to bounce back from these big new emotions. Every time someone validates their emotions, comforts them, and helps them recover, their brains build stronger pathways back to joy from their upset emotions.

Ideally, a child will be helped to recover so often that their brain builds something like a series of highways connecting the joy centers in the front of their brain to the various parts of their lower brain where they feel upset emotions. When these joy pathways develop and get strong, it can become normal for a child to be able to bounce back from all sorts of negative emotions in 90 seconds or less. So, how do joy pathways develop? The answer is a simple process psychologist Jim Wilder calls VCR.[8]

VCR

The process for building these "joy pathways" in the brain can be remembered as VCR—Validate, Comfort, Recover. We will have more to say about how this works later in the book but want to introduce it to you here. Validation happens when parents and other adults meet little ones in their big emotions and provide a safe, calm presence. We share their upset emotion with them. With infants, this has to be done non-verbally.

8 | Marcus Warner and Jim Wilder, *Rare Leadership* (Chicago: Moody 2016) pp. 168-171.

For example, I (Marcus) watched my dad comfort my daughter when she was a baby. She was crying really hard, but Grandpa picked her up and validated her emotions. He looked her in the eyes and imitated her upset emotion by sticking out his bottom lip, making a sad face, and saying in a soothing voice, "What a sad story!" He then began to gently bounce her on his knee and tickle her under chin until she stopped crying and soon started laughing. The whole process took about two minutes. By validating her emotions and comforting her, he helped her recover. As a result, her brain began to form a pathway from sadness back to joy. The more often she experienced that VCR pattern when she was sad, the bigger and faster the pathway between sadness and joy grew.

VCR needs to be reinforced at every stage of development. Before a child learns language, they can still be validated in their emotion, comforted, and helped to return to safe, calm, and connected. Every time a baby cries and a trusted caregiver is able to pick them up, identify with the overwhelming emotion, and whisper, "It's going to be okay," as they pat the child on the back, the child is building neuropathways back to safe, calm, and connected.

SAD-SAD: Learning to name emotions

As the baby grows into a toddler and starts to use their words. It will become important that the child is able to name what they are feeling and express themselves in healthy, age-appropriate ways. This can be difficult at first. If you have ever been around a two-year-old throwing a temper tantrum then you know what it looks like when a child is feeling big emotions and doesn't have the skill to express themselves well. Instead of shaming the child, however, the parent can help by modeling healthy emotional expression and by teaching the child to name what they are feeling.

Naming emotions helps to normalize them. Normalizing emotions is important to validating them. Everyone has feelings. They are part of being human. Emotions come and go like the weather. They are not good or bad, but they may feel good or bad. Feelings color our world in ways that impact everything we do.

Just like the colors of a rainbow, there is a broad spectrum of feelings, and they can vary in intensity. Some emotions—like fear and anger—are high energy. They unleash hormones and chemicals that make it feel like someone has stepped on the gas and revved up our emotional engine. Other emotions—like sadness, shame, and despair—deplete our energy. They can make it feel like someone has slammed on the brakes so that we don't feel like doing anything.

Feeling emotions without being able to name them is like swimming with one arm. It can be a struggle to make any progress in bouncing back from the way we feel. One tool we find helpful we call SAD-SAD. It is a list of six core negative emotions that everyone feels.

Dr. Jim Wilder has identified what can be called "the big six negative emotions." These are right-brain generated emotions. This means they are reactionary and happen faster than thought. By way of contrast, there are left-brain generated emotions that are driven by beliefs. For example, fear is a right-brain reaction to a perceived threat. It is a direct result of our fight, flight, or freeze center getting triggered. Anxiety, on the other hand, is a left-brain reaction to what we believe. It is related to our imagination. Anxiety comes from imaginig a scary future. That anxiety can grow to panic or dread when the scary future we imagine feels inevitable.

In *The 4 Habits of Joy-Filled Marriages*, Chris Coursey and I (Marcus) call these big six negative emtions SAD-SAD emotions to make them easier to remember.[9] For our

---

9 | pp. 75-76

purposes here, we will look at these emotions from both a right-brain and a left-brain perspective.

The right brain generates these emotions when there are triggers related to our attachments/connections. The left brain generates similar emotions when there are problems with our beliefs.

When our connections don't create joy, they tend to create one or more of these six feelings. For example, if I walk in the door and notice that you don't seem happy to see me, I can feel sad before I have time to consciously think about what is happening. Once I start thinking about it, I may believe that you are definitely not happy to see me and perhaps feel shame as well. This may even trigger hopeless despair if I feel like this is a pattern that is impossible to change. Beliefs and connections (attachments) can both contribute to these core emotions.

- » **Sadness**: I have lost something that brought me joy (an object, a relationship, a dream, etc.).

- » **Anxiety** (or fear): I am in danger, or I believe I am in danger. Fear is a right-brain reactionary response to danger. Anxiety is a left-brain response to the fear we imagine, whether it is true or not.

- » **Despair**: My situation is hopeless. Resolution looks impossible.

- » **Shame**: I don't bring you joy. There is something bad about who I am. I feel like hanging my head and hiding.

- » **Anger**: I want injustice or pain to stop. (I want you to stop using that tone with me; I want this feeling to end; I want to stop that mom from treating her child poorly).

- » **Disgust**: Related to the sensation of needing to vomit— it's the feeling that makes you want to say, "Yuck!" I look down on someone or something and feel like avoiding them.

Learning to use these words to name emotions is an important part of validating yourself and others.

A JOY WORKOUT

At the end of each chapter we will provide some sample exercises you can do to start building bounce. You can think of it as a joy workout plan. Since this was the introductory chapter, and you learned a little bit of everything, we won't overwhelm you and ask you to practice something related to all of the ABCs. We will start with appreciation.

Take a 5-minute joy break.

Now and then I'll catch myself noticing how beautiful the sky is or how much I am enjoying something in my environment, but then I keep on going instead of taking a five-minute joy break to simply soak in the moment.

Make it your goal this week to take a five-minute joy break twice each day. Here is a suggested pattern to follow.

During your first joy break, think of a memory that makes you happy. Here are some questions that may help you engage with the memory.

1. Where were you?
2. What was the weather (or the atmosphere, if inside) like?
3. What do you remember about the way you felt?
4. What sensations did you feel in your body?
5. Who else was there?
6. What happened?
7. How does it feel to go back and relive that experience?

During your second joy-break, notice something in your environment that you like. It might be a picture, a decoration, the view out of the window, children playing—whatever you notice that makes you smile. Take a minute or two and just enjoy looking at it, then draw a picture of it or write about your experience and thank God for the little joys in life.

To take this a step further, it helps increase joy and build connection to share our joy with others. Consider calling someone or meeting with someone to tell them about your experience.

LOOKING AHEAD

The next chapter will introduce the idea of emotional capacity and how it develops. We will then explore some basic brain science and the attachment theory that helps us understand how we build bounce. Chapters 4-8 will then explore the ABCs in greater detail, providing a number of exercises you can use both for your own growth and for working with others.

The good news is that wherever you are starting this journey, growth is possible. People used to believe we were victims of the wiring in our brains. We now know that our brains can be rewired. We want to help you learn how to train your brain by building habits that increase your ability to bounce back from the hard things in life.

BEHIND THE ABCS

"ABC" is an attempt to simplify five core habits or skill sets that help us build bounce. These skill sets are:

1. **Quieting** – The number one predictor of good emotional health is the ability to quiet. Quieting is about learning how to calm our bodies and minds after they have been triggered and learning how to practice being quiet without the need for distraction on a regular basis.

2. **Appreciating** – The fastest way to grow joy is to practice appreciation. We do this by training ourselves to dwell on what there is to enjoy in life and sharing that joy with others. This goes beyond saying thank you to taking five minutes or more to soak in the feeling of joy and appreciation.

3. **Thinking** – Beliefs drive left-brain emotions. When our thought life is out of control, our emotions are generally out of control as well. Quieting our minds from racing thoughts, replacing negative thoughts, and learning how to dwell on life-giving thoughts are crucial skills for building bounce.

4. **Forming joy bonds with people** – Just as left-brain emotions are driven by beliefs, so right-brain emotions are driven by our attachments. Instead of joy, too many of us bond with other people in fear, which keeps us disconnected and alone with our troubled emotions.

5. **Forming a joy bond with God** – It is not uncommon for people to form a fear bond with God that causes them to avoid Him or focus on performing for Him rather than actually connecting with Him. A strong joy bond with God means you will never be alone with any emotional pain you have to endure.

We have combined quieting and appreciation into a single skill because they work together to form a single experience. Appreciation can help you quiet, and quieting can make it easier to feel appreciation. We also combined forming joy bonds with God and others into the single idea of building healthy connections. We hope the ABC acronym will make it easier for you to remember and practice these five skills.

CHAPTER TWO
How much weight can you handle?

In the late 1980s and early 90s scientists built something called the Biosphere 2. It was intended to simulate Earth's ecosystem, so they could experiment on nature without destroying it. However, not everything went as predicted. One of the unexpected problems that occurred related to the trees. They grew faster than trees in the wild would normally grow. They also didn't grow strong and hard like normal trees. As a result, they collapsed before they reached maturity. They didn't have the strength to handle their own weight.

Perplexed at first, the scientists eventually came to the conclusion the trees were collapsing because their controlled ecosystem had no wind.[1] This study and others like it have shown that trees need wind, storms, rain and, in some cases, even fire in order to grow strong and become fully mature. Do you think there might be a good life-lesson there somewhere!

WEIGHT

Our emotional capacity is determined by how much emotional weight we can carry. Just as the trees fell over because they lacked the capacity to handle their own weight, so people can fall apart emotionally when their burdens get too heavy. Sometimes the solution is to lighten our load and learn how to take more breaks.

---

1 | Anupum Pant, "The Role of Wind in a Tree's Life" at awesci.com/the-role-of-wind-in-a-trees-life.

One of my favorite pictures shows a donkey hauling a cart full of boxes and overstuffed bags. However, the donkey is not really hauling the load, the load is hauling the donkey. The weight of all the baggage literally has him suspended in midair with all four hooves off the ground! It doesn't matter how hard that donkey tries, he is never going to have the capacity to handle that much weight. Lightening the load is the only solution to his problem. Some of us are in a similar setting. We all need to learn how to put up boundaries and take breathers in order to live within our capacity.

No one has unlimited capacity, so we all need the help that comes from "leaning into God" and walking alongside others. The good news is that the help that comes from such connections helps us grow our capacity.

Years ago, I (Marcus) heard Jim Wilder say, "The most mature person in any room is not necessarily the one with the best credentials or the one with the most impressive title. It is the one who can handle the most weight." I often share this idea with people when I teach and usually see a room full of nodding heads.

Joey and Annie: a capacity parable.

High-joy people have more capacity to handle weight than low-joy people. This is why it is so important to grow our joy. Let's say Joey shows up at kindergarten with the capacity to handle ten pounds of emotional stress. He sits next to Annie who can only handle three pounds of emotional stress.

On the first day of class the teacher enters the room and decides to scare these kids into obeying. She tells them some of the punishments they will experience for disobeying like extra work, notes to parents, and trips to the principal's office. Joey has great parents, so a note home is only slightly stressful. Annie's parents are a different story. It is a truly scary idea to think of her parents getting mad at her. On top of this, Annie doesn't know what a trip to the principal's office involves, but she can imagine really scary things because of her home life. Not only does she have low joy and low emotional capacity, she is predisposed to live with fear. Joey and Annie are not dealing with life with the same level of emotional capacity, are they?

The teacher finishes her speech. For Joey, this experience has created about three pounds of stress. No problem for him. He has the capacity to handle ten pounds of stress. He may feel his blood pressure rise slightly but will have bounced back and feel like himself by the end of the talk. On the other hand, Annie has had a major crisis. First, the speech felt weightier to her than it did to Joey because she lives with so much fear that her imagination took a three-pound event and turned it into a twelve-pound event—more weight than even Joey could have handled.

Secondly, Annie only had the capacity to handle a few pounds of stress to begin with, so this experience has completely overwhelmed her. Her knees are shaking, she has wet herself slightly, she can't concentrate on what is happening in class and is holding her book upside down as she pretends to read. Her fight, flight, or freeze response has been triggered, and she is not going to be able to recover quickly.

For those who are familiar with spiritual warfare, it is probably worth pointing out that this is where the devil tends to show up. He likes to pour the gasoline of shame on the burning fire of fear and overwhelmed emotion. He may whisper the thought, "You've really done it this time. No one else is reacting like this. You better hope no one notices how scared you are, or they are all going to know what a loser you are." He might also nudge Joey or one of the other kids to notice Annie's weakness and make fun of her. He might get one of the kids to announce to the class, "Hey everyone, look at Annie, she's got her book upside down! And –OMG– I think she wet her pants!" Now the whole class is laughing at Annie, and this has just gone to a level twenty stress event. The devil doesn't play fair.

Trauma and Capacity

According to Dr. Jim Wilder, trauma can be defined as anything that stops our emotional capacity from growing. He talks about two kinds of trauma: B Trauma—which is the bad stuff that happens to us like abuse of all sorts—and A Trauma—which is the absence of the good stuff we need like nurture, comfort, and security.

From this perspective, building bounce (growing emotional capacity) requires dealing with trauma. We deal with B Trauma through emotional healing. We deal with A Trauma by developing skills we missed. If, for example, you did not learn to play the piano as a child, you won't have that skill as an adult unless you go through the hard work of building that skill later. If you didn't learn to speak French when you were young, it will be harder to learn it when you are older. You can still learn it when you are older, but you will probably have an accent.

In the same way, "A Trauma" can be thought of as the relational and emotional training we needed but didn't get. Perhaps you had a father who didn't say, "I love you" or who didn't notice you when you were working hard to please him. Maybe your mother was so preoccupied with her own problems she didn't notice yours. Most of us had parents with gaps in their own skill sets. As a result, they couldn't pass on to us what they didn't have.

One of our goals in writing *Building Bounce* is to give you a clear pathway for beginning to learn the skills you may have missed or that may have been underdeveloped. This is where the ABCs come in. Growing the habit of appreciation, uprooting faulty beliefs, and building strong connections with God and others is your pathway to rebuilding or strengthening what you missed growing up.

THE LIFE MODEL

Throughout this book, we refer to Dr. Jim Wilder, Shepherd's House, and the Life Model. Let us introduce you to them briefly and take a quick look at the maturity model they teach.

Shepherd's House was a counseling center in Van Nuys, California that started as a coffee house to reach street kids. Jim Wilder (Ph.D. in Psychology) was one of the lead counselors and eventually became executive director. They built a large team that included people like Jane Willard (Dallas Willard's wife), Anne Bierling, James Friesen, and Maribeth Poole. Under Dr. Wilder's guidance, they developed a model of maturity development based on the latest attachment theory coming out of brain science and related it to their own experiences.

Eventually, the counseling center transitioned into a training ministry and changed its name to Life Model Works. Here is a brief overview of the five stages of maturity as taught by the Life Model.[2]

» **Infancy** (birth to weaning). During infancy, babies need to build a joy foundation for life. By the time they reach the age of four they should have a good capacity for joy and lots of experience at returning to joy from upsetting emotions.

» **Childhood** (weaning to puberty). Childhood is devoted to growing wisdom. During this stage of maturity, a child learns to take care of one person—me. A child needs to learn how they fit into the larger story of life

---

2 | For good resources on the Life Model visit lifemodelworks.org and read *The Complete Guide to Living with Men* by Jim Wilder and *Living from the Heart Jesus Gave You.*

and family, how to care for their basic needs, what brings satisfaction, and how to work for and wait for what is good. By the time they reach puberty, they should have a clear sense of who they are, who their people are, and how to take care of themselves.

» **Adulthood** (puberty to parenthood). Each transition (from Infant to Child, from Child to Adult, etc.) is a form of death and resurrection. A child must die to being an infant. In fact, most young children will tell you quite emphatically, "I am NOT a baby!" The transition from child to adult is a crucial one. Young men and women need to be welcomed into the world of adults by adults who have helped prepare them for this stage of life. At the adult level, people learn to care for their group. The source of their identity shifts from parents to peers. They learn how to be just and merciful in their relationships. They grow their capacity to survive and thrive in the world of adults.

» **Parenthood** (first child to empty nest). After several years of living as an adult, it is time for a new challenge—giving life to a family of your own and guiding your own children to maturity. Parents must selflessly and sacrificially do what is best for their children—not necessarily what their children want, but what is good for them.

» **Elder years** (empty nest to death). The final stage of life begins when your youngest child becomes an adult (you may not be a true empty nester, but you are getting close). The role of the elder is to fill holes in the community. Elders notice people who are falling through the cracks and make sure they are provided for. They provide wisdom, perspective, and stability to a community as those who have weathered many storms.

This model represents what ought to happen spontaneously in an ideal setting. However, trauma (A and B) interrupts this process for everyone. No one lives in a perfect family or goes through life unscathed. Trauma creates holes in our maturity development that need to be repaired as we get older. It can also stagnate our maturity development so that we end up stuck living like emotional infants or emotional children even though we are the age to be a parent or an elder.

Much of my thinking on building bounce has its roots in my relationship with Dr. Wilder and the folks at Life Model Works, and I (Marcus) thought it would be helpful for you to have this introduction to their approach to maturity development.

Parenting: building a healthy emotional immune system

Parents who want their children to grow healthy and strong need to raise kids who can weather storms and wind. This is not easy. Parents are often torn between two extremes. On the one side are parents who want to bubble wrap their kids and keep them from experiencing pain of any kind. On the other extreme, you have parents who try to "toughen up" their kids by giving them adult responsibilities way too soon. Both extremes can be perilous to the heart of a child.

When my children were little, I (Stefanie) spent a lot of time and energy trying to protect them from germs. I would wipe down grocery carts and restaurant tables. I would have them wash their hands after preschool or time spent in the church nursery. I could feel my anxiety rise when other moms talked about the latest virus or strep going around.

I was tired of the constant anxiety I felt about my children's safety so, as a Christian, I did the only thing I knew to do—I prayed. That's when this thought dropped into my head: I needed to shift my focus. Instead of trying to protect them from every threat that might come their way, I needed to focus on building their immune systems. This way, when (not *if*) the germs came their way, they would have the strength to fight them. This thought brought me peace, and I immediately felt my breathing grow deeper and my shoulders relax. The idea of building my children's immune system felt way more manageable than trying to eradicate every germ from their lives.

Building bounce is a lot like building your body's immune system. Instead of avoiding emotions and the situations that cause them, we want to learn how to deal with them and bounce back so we feel like ourselves more quickly.

One day my daughter got in the car after school. With tears in her eyes she told me that a little girl she tried to play with at recess had run away from her. Her pain broke my heart. I started a quiet rant at God for allowing this to happen.

However, I felt the Father's gentle words straight to my heart: "Do you trust Me with Taylor's heart?"

"Yes, Lord, but she feels rejected. We all know how painful that is."

He replied, "Yes, for a moment Taylor felt rejected, but I never left her side, and today she learned compassion."

We live in a broken and fallen world. Because of this, we will experience pain and suffering. But God is able to take our pain and suffering and bring beauty from the ashes. Whether you have experienced big adversity or small, He is the author of redemption. He is able to use it to produce the good fruit of strength from weakness, compassion from pain, joy in trial, and light in the darkness. This is one of the many paradoxes of life in Christ.

The Lord then reminded me of how butterflies must struggle as they break free from their chrysalis. If not allowed to struggle, the butterfly will not develop the wing strength to fly. The Lord asked me to trust Him with my daughter's heart. He knows who He created her to be and exactly what she needed to experience in order to grow into that beautiful and strong young woman.

I wanted to emotionally bubble wrap my children to protect them from adversity. God wanted to use the adversity to grow their emotional capacity. This was the first of many lessons God would teach me about trusting Him with my children.

BUILDING BOUNCE IS A LOT LIKE BUILDING YOUR BODY'S IMMUNE SYSTEM.

A big part of parenting is helping our children build bounce by growing their capacity and strengthening their emotional immune system. Children who learn that they can experience hardship and still be okay will be less afraid, more adventurous, and better equipped to live a full life. Children who don't learn how to experience hard situations and bounce back grow into adults who are generally trapped in avoidance, anger, anxiety, and addiction.

It is important to note that we are not saying parents should intentionally expose their children to hardship. Lifting weights in age- and strength-appropriate ways builds strength, but too much weight too soon can be very destructive. Life is full of plenty of adversity without creating it. On the contrary, a parent's job is to walk alongside their child, lending the parent's emotional capacity to the child as the child grows strength to carry more and more. Lifting too much weight without the proper training will result in injury.

It is also important to note that no one has infinite capacity except God. All of us run out of emotional capacity at some level and get overwhelmed. It is at times like this that God wants us to learn how to lean into His capacity to get through the hardships of life.

The goal of this book is not to help you become super-human so that nothing ever feels like it is too much for you. The goal is to help you learn how to increase your ability to handle hard things and how to pass on those skills to others, whether as a parent, a teacher, a friend, or a leader.

Learning to lean into God's emotional capacity when we are weak and depending on Him to walk us through the hard things in life is also an important component of bounce. Just as we walk with our children and loved ones as they train to lift heavier and heavier weights, our heavenly Father walks with us. We will inevitably come to the end of our capacity. Recognizing our dependence on God is the birthplace of true rest.

A JOY WORKOUT

You have probably heard people talk about "sharpening your axe" or self-replenishment. There's a famous lumber-chack adage along the lines of "If I had five minutes for chopping wood I'd spend the first three sharpening my axe."

Many of us are used to the idea of dividing life into sections called "urgent, important, and 'it-can-wait.'" For far too many of us, replenishment falls into the "it-can-wait" category. We would encourage you to bump that up into the "important" sector of your life. In some cases, maybe even "urgent." Here is another exercise you can do to help build more bounce.

Take a five-minute quieting break.

1. <u>Breathe in a square</u>. (We'll describe this exercise again in the chapter on quieting.) Inhale deeply as you count to four in your head. Hold your breath for a count of four. Slowly exhale as you count to four again. Hold your breath for a four count before going around the "square" two more times.

2. <u>Bounce</u>. Do jumping jacks, deep knee bends, or a little jig, whatever gets your body moving. Count to ten while you do this, then pause and do it again.

3. <u>Sing</u> "Joy to the World" or "Happy Birthday." Singing helps activate both sides of your brain, and happy or silly songs can make you smile.

4. <u>Rub your arms while breathing deeply</u>. Place your hands on your shoulders and run them down to your elbow ten times while inhaling and exhaling deeply.

5. <u>Breathe in a square</u>. Repeat step 1.

6. <u>Sit quietly and think about something you enjoy</u>. Refer to Chapter One's Joy Workout for ideas.

LOOKING AHEAD

If you like brain science, you are going to love the next chapter. If you are intimidated by brain science, don't worry, we make it pretty simple. In the next chapter, we are going to explain a few basics of how the nervous system and the brain relate to emotional capacity. You will learn a few simple models that should make it easier to understand some of the science behind joy.

CHAPTER THREE
a basic brain model

In this chapter we want to unpack a basic model of how the brain functions. This is not a deep dive into the details of brain activity but a look at the brain as a machine designed to run on joy. We will introduce one element at a time until we complete a simple diagram.

Line #1 (horizontal)

Conscious

Subconscious

The diagram begins with a simple horizontal line. This line separates the conscious from the subconscious part of your brain. The technical term for what is below the line is "sub-cortical." It is home to the thalamus, the nucleus accumbens, and the amygdala. We will explain those more later.

Above this line, conscious thought on the left side of your brain involves thinking, ideas, and words. Consciousness on the right side of the brain is more about awareness and being synchronized with the world around us. It is connected to the idea of mindfulness.

Below this line, you do not think about what you are doing because activity is happening faster than either conscious thought or conscious synchronization.

For example, when you ride a bike, you can't possibly think about all of the activity that is going into simultaneously viewing your surrounding area, anticipating coming problems, listening for sounds, pedaling, steering, breathing, and everything else your body is doing. The good news is that you don't need to think about all of these things because God has designed your brain to take care of that stuff automatically. Some of it became automatic because you learned skills that became habits (like pedaling and steering a bike). Some of it is automatic because God hardwired the activity into your brain (like seeing, hearing, and smelling, or sending signals from your brain to your legs). All of this subconscious activity is sub-cortical.

This part of the brain is fully functional from the moment you are born. It can still develop and learn skills, but it is functional at birth. The top part of the brain is largely undeveloped and partly unformed at birth. This means the part of the brain that thinks thoughts, uses words, tells stories, experiences joy, and contains our identity is essentially undeveloped. It will have to be grown through training and experience as we interact relationally with the people around us.

Line #2 (vertical)

If you were to open the top of your head and remove your brain, it would naturally fall into two sections—right and left. The vertical line of our diagram represents the division between the right and left hemispheres of the brain. Notice that the two lines form a quadrant of four boxes. In this chapter we will explain what is happening in each of these four sectors of brain function.

The two sides of the brain can be thought of as two engines. Each one uses a completely different operating system. The engine on the right is our relational engine. It is the part of our brain that forms attachments. The engine on the left can be thought of as our narrative engine. It is the part of the brain that forms beliefs and puts those beliefs into a narrative that explains life. The engine on the left uses words and is very concerned with problem solving and damage control. It forms beliefs and spins narratives to help analyze and solve problems. The engine on the right does not use words. It is pre-verbal and serves as the anchor for most of our relational and emotional regulation skills.

Beliefs   **Connections**

According to Scottish psychiatrist Iain McGilchrist, the left side of the brain is about focus, and the right is about universal awareness.[1] He uses the example of a bird to illustrate the left/right difference. Suppose a bird is eating seeds that have fallen among pebbles. He will need great focus to make sure he eats the seeds and not the pebbles. This is a left-brain task. It is a problem-solving and "getting work done" activity. However, the bird must also be alert in case there are predators in the area or family who need him. This is a right-brain activity. While his left brain focuses on getting work done, his right brain is staying relationally engaged with the world around him. These are two completely separate operating systems.

1 | Iain McGilchrist "The Divided Brain" at www.ted.com/talks/Iain_mcgilchrist_the_divided_brain.

Both the left and right side of the brain play a role in emotions. The right side is primarily related to how connections (attachments) affect our emotions. The left side is primarily related to how beliefs impact emotions. This may help you understand where we got the B and the C of the ABCs of building bounce.

Before we go into the four quadrants, it should be pointed out that the brain also has a back and front dimension to it—because it's not flat. One of the primary functions impacted by this is that we tend to experience joy in the front of our brain and upsetting emotions in the back part of our brain. Thus, returning to joy from upsetting emotions involves building pathways from the back of the brain to the front. Our focus, however, will be on the levels of brain function and how they affect our emotions.

Quadrant #1 – (bottom right)
stage one of the relational engine

We experience life as neurons conduct electrical current from our nervous system into the bottom right quadrant of the brain. This is the first part of the brain that interacts with the world around us. It is subconscious—so it happens before we can think about it—and it is related to attachment. This means our first interaction with the world passes through the relational engine of the brain.

**Subconscious
Connections**

It is informative that God designed our brains to be anchored in attachment. Connecting to others is the deepest longing of the soul, and it is reflected in the deepest activity of the brain. It doesn't take a brain scientist to see the relationship between the design of the brain and the importance of love. God made us to be loving people who bond to others in love. This is completely consistent with the idea that the two greatest commandments are to love the Lord your God with all of your heart, soul, mind, and strength, and to love your neighbor as yourself.[2]

ATTACHMENT AND ASSESSMENT

Let's take a closer look at the bottom right quadrant of brain function. It is in this part of the brain you find the attachment center and the assessment center. The attachment center can be thought of as a light bulb that goes on when things are personal to us or when we crave attachment.

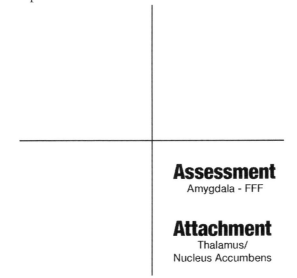

Assessment
Amygdala - FFF

Attachment
Thalamus/
Nucleus Accumbens

2 | Mark 12:28-31. Some people are over eager to make a direct connection between various brain functions and the idea of the heart or the soul or the mind. But these represent something spiritual that is at work in the brain and in the rest of our bodies and should not be reduced to specific elements of the brain.

For example, if you walk up to me at a conference and hold out your hand to greet me, this part of my brain will light up whether I know you or not because you just became personal to me. Immediately a signal is sent to the assessment center to determine whether you are good, bad, or scary. This all happens faster than I have a chance to be consciously aware of it.

My subconscious assessment center can only give three possible answers to the type of attachment it is evaluating. The attachment is either *good*, *bad*, or *scary*. It is this assessment that triggers our fight, flight, or freeze reaction. At a higher level of brain function, I can think my way into different beliefs about this instinctive assessment and act on that, but there is nothing I can do to keep my brain from having this initial reaction.

The assessment center is sometimes called the fight, flight, or freeze (FFF) center. When it feels fear, I want to flee. When it feels anger, I want to fight. When it gets completely overwhelmed, I tend to freeze. Our FFF reactions can be mild and easily overcome. But sometimes they are overwhelming and push us beyond our emotional capacity.

When someone says, "I got triggered," they usually mean their fight, flight, or freeze reaction was bigger than they could handle. When you get triggered, it is easy for the rest of your brain to experience diminished ability to function. It is harder to think clearly when you are overwhelmed. It is harder to feel like yourself. It is harder to get free from negative emotions. Because the attachment/assessment center is foundational to everything above it, it affects everything we do and feel. But if you have a big enough joy center and your pathways back to joy have grown strong enough, things that used to trigger you can stop being triggering.

Joy bonds and fear bonds

Attachment and assessment combine to form either joy bonds or fear bonds. If my brain assesses a person, substance, animal, or experience as bad or scary, a fear bond is created. For example, some people have an instinctive love of dogs. Just seeing a dog makes them happy because their brain created a joy bond with these furry creatures. On the other hand, some people have an instinctive fear of dogs. Their natural reaction to the animals isn't joy but fear because early in life their brain learned to see them as scary.

I (Marcus) happen to have a fear bond to dogs. It doesn't mean I can't enjoy them and play with them, but my brain doesn't register joy just by seeing one either. This is probably related to the fact that I had two different neighbors with very scary dogs that were as tall as me (when I was three) and occasionally barked angrily in my face. Since then, however, I have owned a dog and enjoyed many aspects of having him around, but I never got to the point where there was an instantaneous feeling of joy just from having him around.

According to Dr. Wilder, "fear bonds form as the result of failed attempts at self-preservation."[3] Early experiences in fearful relationships we cannot escape produce powerful internal emotions that can be overwhelming. No one likes to live outside of their emotional capacity for very long, so when this happens, we instinctively learn to start avoiding those emotions and the situations that cause them.

For example, if you have had a bad experience with the IRS, you might find yourself avoiding anything to do with tax preparation. Of course, this simply compounds your problems because your avoidance of the work increases the likelihood of more problems later. If you have had a bad

---

3 | E. James Wilder "Changing Motivation from Fear to Love" at LifeModel.org (2004). http://lifemodel.org/download/Changing%20Fear%20to%20Love.pdf

experience with a teacher, you might avoid doing the homework for that teacher. On the other hand, you might become completely pre-occupied with the homework for that teacher to the point that you neglect your other schoolwork. Both reactions are driven by a fear of emotions you don't want to experience. Neither reaction is anchored in joy. From this perspective, a fear bond is essentially a relationship driven by the need to avoid pain rather than increasing the joy of connection.

Dismissive, distracted, and disorganized

Life Model Works and THRIVEtoday both teach three fundamental types of fear bonds that can form: distracted, dismissive, and disorganized.[4] The assessment center can be thought of as a light bulb. It lights up when something or someone is personal to me. When we are forced to bond with people who are not always safe, it can cause this light bulb to start malfunctioning.

Dismissive attachment is formed because my brain lights up hoping for relational connection, but no one responds. When this happens often enough, my brain learns to ignore and eventually not even notice that the light is coming on. Dismissive people find it hard to form attachments. They can be friendly but have trouble creating "sticky" relationships. In the worst cases, they don't feel any impulse to attach because they have been disconnected from this part of the brain.

Distracted attachment is created because I am expected to "light up" and "turn on" when others need me, but they don't necessarily respond when I need them. As a result, the light bulb in my attachment center stays on most of the

---

4 | Chris Coursey, president of THRIVEtoday, wrote a paper titled "Attachments" when he worked for Life Model Works that lays out the three types of fear bonds that form when attachments develop poorly. This paper can be found online by searching "dismissive, distracted, disorganized."

time, just in case someone needs me to attach. Distracted people are just that—easily distracted. They tend to give their attention to whatever is scariest or whatever demands their attention rather than what deserves their attention. For example, when I (Marcus) was a pastor, I found it hard to say no to people with problems. This created a real problem for my family. I often neglected them because they weren't having problems, so I gave my time to the people in need. This is okay now and then, but over time it started robbing my family of more and more time together. My distracted attachment style was afraid of letting people down and reacting to situations out of that fear rather than being guided by principle or joyful attachment.

Disorganized attachment is created when infants and children have to bond with someone who is frequently scary. They never know when it is safe to bond. When the attachment light comes on, the assessment center says, "Bad and scary. Get away." However, the attachment center is saying, "Get close." This leaves the brain with an unsolvable problem that tends to make things shut down. How do I get close and go away at the same moment? I am experiencing an intolerable conflict. This type of fear bond is called disorganized because the child does not develop an organized personality that remains the same. Instead, their brain remains "disorganized" and they function like different people depending on the emotion or situation in front of them. This is classically related to dissociation and borderline personality disorder.

Addiction

Attachment and assessment also combine to play a powerful role in addiction. An important part of the attachment center is the nucleus accumbens. This is the part of the brain related to pain and pleasure. It is drawn to what brings pleasure and avoids what brings pain. If I learn that connecting with people can be painful but that ice cream brings pleasure, it will be easy to avoid relationships and become addicted to sweets. Addictions are non-relational substitutes for the joyful connection our brains crave. Over time, we will learn to seek out our addiction over relationship. Since this is the deepest part of brain function, you can't simply break addictions by choosing to stop. New attachments have to be formed.

Writing with Jim Wilder, Ed Khouri—an addiction recovery specialist—had this to say about the attachment center and addiction:

> God created the attachment center to attach to him and others in joy-filled and mutually fulfilling relationships. He designed us so that our entire brain functions best in joyful, honest and loving relationships. Without these attachments, the attachment center, and the entire brain function in a state of ongoing emotional and cognitive distress.
>
> In this state of distress, and absence of secure attachment, the brain's attachment center will "latch onto" anything that provides a sense of connection and pleasure.[5]

---

5 | Jim Wilder and Ed Khouri, "What is Addiction?" at lifemodel.org (http://lifemodel.org/download/AddictionAttachmentThriving.pdf)

Quadrant #2: (top right)
stage two of the relational engine

Action
Prefrontal Cortex
(Joy Center)
(Identity Center)

Attunement
Cingulate Cortex
(mother core) ON/OFF
SWITCH

Assessment
Amygdala - FFF

Attachment
Thalamus/
Nucleus Accumbens

The top right quadrant of our diagram relates to the part of our brain that is both relational and conscious. This level of consciousness is different than conscious thought. It is more like awareness. You can be aware of something before you actively think about it. For example, I may be aware that my wife is smiling at me as I read my book before I actively react to that awareness by thinking about it. Once I start thinking about it, a whole new set of possibilities gets set in motion, but much of that process will be determined by whether my bond with my wife is rooted in joy or fear.

The brain operates like an elevator. In our book *Rare Leadership*, Jim and I coined the term "joy elevator" to explain what is happening on the right side of the brain. The brain is like an elevator because it is hierarchical. This means if there is a problem at the attachment/assessment level, everything above that will be affected. If I feel safe, calm, and connected at the attachment/assessment level, the rest of life gets easier. But if my FFF reaction gets triggered, the rest of my brain will have a hard time functioning properly. If I have a joy bond with my wife, it is easier to believe things about her that make me want to have her around. If I am fear bonded with my wife, it is easier to believe things about her that make me want to avoid her or be certain (out of fear) to keep her happy so she doesn't do damage to my emotional state.

If I have a joy bond with my wife, it is easier to act like myself around her. But if I have a fear bond or if I get triggered by an FFF reaction, it can be almost impossible to act like myself. Instead, I may shut down, melt down, or blow up.

The ON/OFF Switch

The FFF reaction that happens in the assessment center can cause the attunement center to go offline.[6] When this happens, the top part of the right hemisphere does not get access to what is happening. Because of this, the part of my brain that remembers who I am and how to act like myself never gets access to the information. Instead, my brain activity jumps to the left hemisphere. If you were to scan this activity in the brain, you would see a dark patch where the identity center is rather than seeing it lit up.

In this sense, you have an on/off switch in your brain. When it is on, your relational circuits stay engaged, and the top part of your brain that remembers who you are and how it is like you to act has a chance to guide your reactions. If the switch goes off, your relational circuits go off, and you act like a different person. One of the most important lessons we can learn from brain science is the importance of keeping our relational circuits on when we get stressed.

---

6 | When we get shut down at Level 2 (amygdala), this can result in dissociation and memory amnesia. However, when we get shut down at Level 3 (cingulate cortex), we remember the trauma, but our relational circuits still go offline.

ATTUNEMENT AND ACTION

The action center is the key to maturity and emotional capacity. It is the part of our brain that remembers who we are, so we could call it our identity center. This center is located just behind the right eye. Now and then you will hear stories of people who sustain an injury to this part of their brain that completely changes their personality.

I (Marcus) spoke with a man recently who had a brain tumor removed that significantly damaged the right part of his brain. You could actually see the right side of his head slightly curved in where part of the brain had been removed. He explained to me that his left-brain skills were still intact and thus he excelled at his engineering job, but his attachments and emotions had been profoundly altered. Reading about the brain in *The 4 Habits of Joy-Filled Marriages* helped him understand why his personality had changed so profoundly and gave him hope that new joy could be developed.

Our sense of identity is primarily grown in relationship. We see ourselves as part of a group. The more clearly we know who our people are, the more developed our sense of identity will be. If I see myself as a man, that puts me in a group. My identity will be formed by what I believe it means to be a man and by the type of attachment I feel with other men. Attachment and identity are directly related. I will feel like I belong to the people with whom I feel the greatest attachment. They are my group—my people—my tribe.

One of the goals of discipleship is to help people form a new identity in Christ. To do this they need more than information about who they are in Christ (though this is very important). They need to belong to a group who take their identity from Christ and begin to see these people as 'my people.'

We also find this principle in addiction recovery. People often get sober while they are in a center and surrounded by people who are working toward a common goal. But when they get released, they go back to their old group. It is very difficult to maintain a new identity when you are living with the people who gave you your old identity. Changing who your people are is an important part of recovery.

THE ATTUNEMENT CENTER

At birth, the attachment center is fully formed, which means infants come out of the womb wanting to attach. The assessment center is also fully formed, which means they can feel fear and anger immediately. On day one, their attunement center is partially formed, but it will grow to be fully formed over the next year as it interacts with its primary care giver (usually mom). The attunement center is attached to mother and soon begins to download mommy's brain by watching how she reacts to her world. If mommy is full of joy and synchronizes quickly with the baby's needs, the infant will develop a stable sense of well-being. But if mommy is preoccupied, anxious, and easily angry, the baby will download a brain that is wired to see the world through that lens.

When the attunement center gets a "bad" or "scary" message from the assessment center, it will often derail our brain function so that the next level of brain function—our action center—doesn't get the information it should. When that happens, we can't act like ourselves because the part of our brain that remembers who we are is offline. For the same reasons, we will also have a hard time living out of joy rather than fear.

The top-right quadrant of this diagram represents the part of our brain that runs the show. In engineering terms, it is the master cylinder that controls the 'slave' cylinders. For example, when you step on the brake pedal in your car, you activate the master cylinder. That master cylinder sends hydraulic fluid to the 'slave' cylinders so they press the brake pads against the wheels. The master makes sure everything operates in a coordinated manner. If the master cylinder is offline or non-functional, you are going to have some serious problems stopping your car. In the same way, the action center of the brain is like the brain's master cylinder. If it is functioning properly, everything else will work well. You will think better, speak better, solve problems better—everything your left brain does will improve because your left brain follows the right brain like a slave cylinder follows a master cylinder.[7]

Quadrant #3: (left hemisphere) stage one of the narrative engine

Narrative
Conscious
Left Prefrontal
Cortex

Action
Prefrontal Cortex
(Joy Center)
(Identity Center)

Attunement
Cingulate Cortex
(mother core)

Assessment
Amygdala - FFF

Attachment
Thalamus/
Nucleus Accumbens

---

7 | I (Marcus) learned this principle from Jim Wilder when we were working on *Rare Leadership*.

We often call quadrant three the <u>narrative engine</u>. The top part of the left hemisphere of the brain is where we generate words, concepts, and stories to explain life. In the ABCs of building bounce, it is the part of the brain most directly related to our beliefs. This part of the brain is where we

» analyze situations,

» solve problems,

» explain experiences, and

» verbalize thoughts.

It is the part of the brain designed to focus on tasks. This is why it's hard to focus on solving problems (like answering emails) and get interrupted. The relational part of the brain is often not as engaged while you focus on a task.

One of the main tasks of the narrative engine[8] is to explain reality. It takes the information it is given and tries to make sense out of it. Narratives are powerful forces when it comes to relationships and emotions. This is why the devil—as the father of lies (John 8:44)—is so committed to deception. If he can control our narrative, he can run our lives. We will have more to say about this in the chapter on beliefs.

The arrow in the diagram represents the flow of energy through the brain. Electrical current enters the brain in the bottom right quadrant, flows to the top of the right side of the brain, then moves over to the left hemisphere where it is interpreted in quadrant #3—the narrative engine. After this it flows out of the brain and back into our nervous system through quadrant #4.

---

8 | Psychiatrist Karl Lehman refers to the narrative engine as the VLE – verbal logical explainer. Its job is to provide explanations of the world around us. See *Outsmarting Yourself* (This Joy Books, 2011), p. 23.

Quadrant #4: (left hemisphere) stage two of the narrative engine

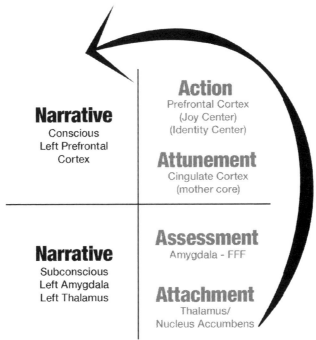

Just as there are attachment-based emotions generated on the right side of the brain, so there are belief-based emotions generated on the left. The beliefs created by the narrative engine in quadrant #3 create an emotional reaction in quadrant #4. When people say beliefs drive feelings, they are referring to the feelings generated in this lower quadrant of the left side of the brain.

If you were to look at the two halves of your brain, they would look identical. One side mirrors the other. Thus, the top of the left and right hemispheres both have a prefrontal cortex. Below that, both have a cingulate cortex. At the subcortical level, both have an amygdala and a thalamus. The difference is one of function and the fact that the right brain gets the information first and acts on it before the left brain can engage. One of the main points we are trying to make about the way the brain works is that we need both hemispheres to be functioning well in order to experience peak emotional capacity.

Different interventions are needed for attachment-based emotions and belief-based emotions. With beliefs, we have to change our narrative. With attachments, we need more relational interventions. To understand how this works, it can be helpful to understand your brain's pain processing pathway.

THE PAIN PROCESSING PATHWAY

Suffering becomes trauma when we feel alone in it. In order for suffering to keep from becoming traumatic, our brain needs to process the pain at all five levels of function: 1) attachment, 2) assessment, 3) attunement, 4) action, and 5) narrative. In his book *Outsmarting Yourself*, psychiatrist Karl Lehman refers to these five levels of brain function as "the pain processing pathway."[9] If our pain completes the journey so that we do not feel alone in our suffering and we arrive at a satisfying explanation of what happened, suffering does not become traumatic. Or, if it was already traumatizing, completing that journey can bring healing.

Severe trauma generally has two key components to it: 1) I feel all alone in my pain, 2) I have no satisfying explanation for my experience. As the experienced trauma recovery specialist Melissa Finger points out, intense childhood trauma is often related to pain and intolerable conflict.[10] When I feel alone in my pain and trapped in intolerable conflict[11]

---

9 | Karl Lehman, *Outsmarting Yourself* (Evanston: This Joy! Books, 2011) p. 1.

10 | Melissa Finger, *Trauma Coping System: Dissociation as a Response to Pain and Intolerable Conflict* (Seek First Ministries, 2018).

11 | When you have intolerable conflict you also have disorganized attachment.

because there is no satisfying explanation for my experience, I am trapped in trauma. Healing happens when both of those issues experience resolution. The most common way we have seen this happen is through a direct intervention by Jesus during inner healing prayer.[12] When Jesus meets someone in a painful memory, they are no longer alone with their pain—Jesus is with them. Jesus is also able to do or say things that allow them to be set free from the inner conflict. Sometimes the satisfying answer is as simple as, "You are going to be okay" or "You'll understand in the next life." But sometimes He gives entirely new perspectives on our experiences.

One of the first times I (Marcus) heard of Jesus healing a painful memory in this way was in the ministry of Dr. David Seamands.[13] He told the story of a woman who was trapped in the emotions surrounding an abortion. She was haunted by the memory of being alone in a hotel room with her dead baby. Dr. Seamands led her to invite Jesus into that memory. When He came, He picked up the baby, wrapped him in His robes, and started to walk toward the door. Just before He got to the door, Jesus stopped, looked at the woman and smiled and showed her a baby who was very much alive in His arms. This experience took away her sense of being alone with her pain and gave her the satisfying narrative that she would be reunited with her child one day and that Jesus had forgiven her and still loved her deeply.

When the four levels of your joy elevator are operating well, you can process pain quickly and efficiently. It is much easier for your narrative engine to come up with a satisfying explanation of your experience when the right brain sys-

---

12 | For more about inner healing and stories about how Jesus can bring healing to painful memories, see *Understanding the Wounded Heart* or *REAL Prayer* by Marcus Warner.

13 | I heard this story on a cassette tape in the early 1990s but do not have access to it for definitive reference.

tems are operating properly. However, if you have problems at any of the five levels, you can get stuck in your pain.

» Level one is home to the deepest pain a human can feel. It is called "attachment pain." If the elevator gets stuck here, you can feel like you are falling apart completely and have no capacity to deal with life.

» Level two pain can cause your brain to send a constant flow of adrenaline through your body that keeps you in a state of anxiety (scary) or anger (bad). When this happens, it can be almost impossible to relax and feel peace.

» Level three pain can cause you to misread people, which can lead to making foolish decisions about the way you interact with them. You may ignore someone who deserves your attention, or you may get upset with someone who has done nothing wrong.

» Level four pain leaves you forgetting how it is like you to act, and you can end up handling people and problems in a way that "isn't you." Instead of being relational, you can easily go into enemy mode and concern yourself only with damage control as you interact with people.

» Level five refers to the narrative engine. When our core problem is our beliefs, they need to get corrected in order to make progress.

Each of these levels requires a different type of intervention if you are trying to help someone bounce back from where they are stuck. They also require a different type of intervention if you are looking to help yourself recover.

» **Level One:** Share. At the attachment level, people just need someone to be there, to be happy to be with them, and to not leave them alone. They need someone to share the experience. You might think of Job's friends before they started to talk. They spent seven days just sitting in silence with him and sharing the pain.

» **Level Two**: <u>Soothe</u>. Since level two (assessment) is about high-energy emotions like anger and fear, when people are stuck there they need someone to meet them in those emotions and help soothe those emotions by quieting with them.

» **Level Three**: <u>Support</u>. At level three (attunement) people may need supportive action. You can think of this as the "Let's do this together" level. You may go with someone to the bus station or walk with them to school. In a child therapy session, you might sit down and draw a picture together.

When my (Marcus's) son was about seven, he found a stray cat. The scene was adorable. He came inside the house early on a cold winter night, all bundled in his down coat and holding a tiny cat in his arms. Looking up with pleading eyes, he uttered those classic words, "Daddy, can we keep him?" As an adult, I knew all of the other issues that went with saying yes and knew my son would not be able to do this by himself. However, once his older sister and his mother also fell in love with the furry visitor, I told my son, "Okay, we can keep the cat for the night. But tomorrow we have to ask our neighbors if anyone knows about him. He may already have a family."

The next day, my son and I went door to door near the spot where he had found the kitten. I didn't just send him on his own. I showed active support by going with him so that he could see what it looked like to be responsible and practice. We only had to knock on three doors before we found the owner. To our great delight, the young couple had rescued him despite their allergies and were actually looking for a family to take him. They even offered to help pay for his shots and neutering. If that is not a sign from God, I don't know what is. We kept the cat. I was also able to support my son by tuning into his emotions and helping him learn how to act like himself and do the right thing.

» **Level Four**: <u>Show</u>. The joy elevator does not learn with words. It is comprised primarily of mirror neurons that learn by observing. One of the ways I learn how to respond to anger is by watching how other people do it. If I have grown up with nothing but immature models of handling anger, it may be impossible for my brain to envision any other way of dealing with it without introduction to new models. If I can watch a mature person handle anger in a relational way, the mirror neurons on the right side of my brain can observe and learn. One of the keys to developing the top level of our brain function is getting to watch as more mature people than us show us how it is like a mature person to act.

» **Level Five**: <u>Suggest</u>. The fifth level of brain function happens on the left side of the brain in the narrative engine. When this is where we are stuck, the proper solution is suggesting a new narrative or a different explanation of reality. This intervention does no good if we are stuck at a deeper level, but if this is where the problem is, providing new information that revises the narrative can help people change their beliefs and finish processing their pain.

Chris Coursey, who co-authored the book *The 4 Habits of Joy-Filled Marriages* with me (Marcus), illustrates these levels of intervention with the story of how he helped his wife deal with an FFF experience. They were in Michigan and decided to climb to the top of a lighthouse. The problem was that Chris's wife had a fear of heights. Halfway up she got triggered and froze. Chris's first reaction was to make a suggestion. "We are halfway there. You've done great so far. It is going to be okay, why don't we keep going." That didn't help. It was not the part of her brain that was stuck. Next he tried showing her what to do. "Look," he said, "put one foot in front of the other like this. We can do this one step at a time." No response. So, he went down to intervention #3—sharing. He offered to hold her hand and go up the steps together so they could share the experience. That didn't work either. He then sat down next to her and helped her get her breathing under control and spent some time sitting and quieting until she felt like herself again. Once she was able to soothe her upset emotions, her joy elevator reengaged, and she was able to act like herself and finish climbing up the stairs.

A JOY WORKOUT

We talked about the importance of keeping your relational circuits on. I know of one couple who turned this challenge into a game. When they find themselves getting tense with one another, they give a prize—not to the one who wins the argument—but to the one who gets their relational circuits back online faster. As part of your joy workout program, you might do something similar. Even if you aren't married or don't have a partner to do this with, you can offer yourself some sort of prize for recognizing when your relational circuits have shut down and getting them back on.

Compare and Contrast

Think about a time you tried to talk through a problem while your relational circuits were on, and contrast that with a time you tried to talk through a problem while your circuits were off.

1. What differences did you notice in your breathing?
2. What differences did you notice in the results?
3. What did you emotionally feel when you were done with the conversation?
4. How did your body feel when you were done with the conversation?
5. What helped you keep your relational circuits on?
6. What made it hard to keep them on?
7. Any lessons learned?

LOOKING AHEAD

It is time to start diving into the actual practice of the ABCs of building bounce. In the first three chapters, we have looked at the theory and science behind the practices, now we want to help you learn how to put into practice the habits that build bounce. We will start with quieting. Learning how to quiet your body and your mind is one of the most important skills required for building bounce.

CHAPTER FOUR
quieting

You may have noticed that babies like to build joy! They instinctively look for a face with eyes that are happy to see them. Once they make eye contact with those sparkling eyes, they start to feel joy. They can giggle and laugh and play as they experience more and more joy. But, at some point, they will look away. This doesn't mean they don't like the person. It means the part of their brain that fills up with joy has reached its capacity and they need to rest. Give them a few minutes of quiet, and they will soon be back for more.

It is important for babies to get both joy and quiet. If people don't understand this, they may try to force the infant to keep smiling and laughing when they really need a break. This actually overwhelms the child because it prevents them from getting the break they need. When adults get in sync with babies and build joy with them when they are ready for joy, and give them a break when they are ready to rest, babies get a really good joy workout that grows the joy center in their brains.

This isn't just true for babies. It remains true for our entire lives. A good joy workout of appreciation and quiet will continue to grow the joy center in your brain for as long as you live. Our need for joy and rest never ends. People who build strong habits around quieting and appreciation lay a strong foundation for emotional resilience.

QUIETING AND APPRECIATION

As we have stated, building bounce requires three core elements: Appreciation, Beliefs, and Connections. Appreciation grows your joy and trains your brain to look for what there is in life to enjoy rather than what there is to fear. Appreciation is related to quieting. They work together like a joy workout program to grow the joy center in your brain. Sometimes quieting is needed in order to practice appreciation, and sometimes appreciation is needed in order to quiet.

In *The 4 Habits of Joy-Filled Marriages*, Chris Coursey tells the story of how practicing appreciation helped his wife Jen quiet her mind and body so she could sleep.[1] It was not uncommon for Chris to fall asleep while his wife stayed awake and restless for more than an hour. Her restlessness would wake him up, and they would both be frustrated.

In desperation, they decided to try an experiment and practice an appreciation exercise after getting in bed. They would tell each other three things they appreciated from their day, three things they appreciated about God, and three things they appreciated about each other. The exercise took ten to fifteen minutes and helped them both quiet. Going to sleep after being quieted with joy makes for deeper, more satisfying sleep. Whereas falling asleep in a state of anxiety can actually kill brain cells as you sleep.[2] For Chris and Jen, practicing appreciation helped them quiet.

On the other hand, sometimes you need to quiet before you can practice appreciation. Many times I (Marcus) have tried to "fix" my upset emotions by diving straight into ap-

---

1 | Marcus Warner and Chris Coursey, *The 4 Habits of Joy-filled Marriages* (Chicago: Northfield, 2019) 95-98.

2 | See Rebecca Bernstein, "The Mind and Mental Health: How Stress Affects the Brain" at https://www.tuw.edu/health/how-stress-affects-the-brain/ (July 26, 2016). For a helpful explanation of the brain and anxiety see, Dr. John Kenworthy "Your Brain on Stress and Anxiety" (Nov. 8, 2013). https://www.youtube.com/watch?v=gmwiJ6ghLIM

preciation only to discover that it was impossible to do the exercises until I quieted first.

SOMETIMES YOU NEED TO QUIET BEFORE YOU CAN PRACTICE APPRECIATION.

Since quieting and appreciation are both essential elements of a good joy workout, we have decided to use this chapter to introduce the importance of quieting and to provide some simple exercises for you to try so you can begin developing this important habit. In the next chapter we will focus on appreciation and provide tools for helping you build that life-giving habit.

Sabbath

The ability to quiet may be the most important skill we can master when it comes to long-term emotional health. People who can reliably quiet after getting upset have greater emotional stability than those who don't know how to quiet their minds and bodies.

Most of us live distracted lives. We can't sit still for very long without needing to listen to music, watch TV, or play games on our phone. In this high-tech age, it is hard to simply be quiet. Writing in the 1940s A.W. Tozer warned:

> Among the enemies to devotion none is so harmful as distractions. Whatever excites the curiosity, scatters the thoughts, disquiets the heart, absorbs the interests or shifts our life focus from the kingdom of God within us to the world around us—that is a distraction; and the world is full of them. Our science-based civilization has given us many benefits, but it has multiplied our distractions and so taken away far more than it has given.[3]

3 | "Distractions! Distractions! Distractions!!" Tozer Devotional (Sun. June 13, 2021 [sic]) cmalliance.org/devotions/tozer?id=737

If it was that bad in the relatively low-tech days of the mid twentieth century, imagine how hard the struggle is today!

God wanted us to understand how important quiet and rest are by giving us the Sabbath. The Sabbath is meant to be a time of resting from work and attaching to God. It combines quieting and connection.

The scriptural Sabbath starts at 6 pm on Friday evening and ends at 6 pm on Saturday. It is common to start the Sabbath with a meal surrounded by friends and family. Friday afternoons are spent preparing food, wrapping up work for the week, and anticipating the joy of being with people you love as well as taking a break from the normal routine. Synagogue worship involves gathering relationally and spending time reflecting on wisdom from God's Word.

Most people who have not grown up with Sabbath often struggle to build a rhythm of rest. According to the Torah, however, God's people practiced Sabbath 70 days a year! Can you imagine how much more emotional capacity you might have if you could count on 70 days of rest and renewal each year?

Beyond the rhythm created by practicing Sabbath, quieting is also about the ability to calm yourself emotionally after getting stirred up or triggered. We practice quieting by focusing our thoughts on what is good. We do not empty our minds, but we do quiet our minds by stilling our restless thoughts.

Quieting your body

Quieting involves both your body and your brain. Sometimes it is hard to quiet because your thoughts are racing. Sometimes it is hard to quiet because your body is jittery, your breathing is shallow, your muscles are tense, and you have more adrenaline than you need. Calming your body and your brain are both important parts of quieting.

One of the issues involved in quieting your body is that emotions often trigger a physical reaction. Fear and anger send adrenaline through your body and create all sorts of reactions. For example, your face, ears, back, or neck may get hot. Your stomach may get tight or start to burn. Panic can make you feel like you are having a heart attack. The Bible describes people in fear as going limp as if the life has drained out of their bodies.[4] Every emotion affects the body in some way. This is why so many chronic physical problems have their roots in unresolved emotional trauma.[5]

Learning to recognize how stress is affecting your body in the moment as it is happening is crucial to regulating your nervous system through quieting. The autonomic nervous system (ANS) includes everything in your body from hormones and chemicals, to neurons, the spinal column, and your brain. Your ANS is what controls your response to stress. It works like driving a car. The sympathetic branch of your nervous system is like a gas pedal, and the parasympathetic branch is like the brake. If you have your foot on the gas too long, your body will experience too much stress, and things will start breaking down. On the other hand, if you have your foot on the brake too often, you will wear down and feel sluggish. A healthy ANS does not over-en-

---

4 | Isaiah 13:7, "Because of this, all hands will go limp, every heart will melt with fear." Jeremiah 6:24, "We have heard reports about them, and our hands hang limp. Anguish has gripped us, pain like that of a woman in labor." Jeremiah 50:43, "The king of Babylon has heard reports about them, and his hands hang limp. Anguish has gripped him, pain like that of a woman in labor." Ezekiel 7:17, "Every hand will go limp; every leg will be wet with urine." All of these passages and more demonstrate the physical reactions that come with overwhelm and especially fear.

5 | For a good summary of the role of emotions in the body, see Bessel van der Kolk, *The Body Keeps the Score: Brain, Mind, and Body in the Healing of Trauma* (Penguin Books, 2015).

gage either system but is able to navigate between them, adapting to the situation at hand so you can engage and recover from the daily stresses of life.

When we feel stress, our bodies will release hormones into the body that are meant to get us moving. When we get where we are going, however, we need the ability to apply the brake so that our nervous system can rest and repair from the exertion. Many people find themselves with either their gas pedal or brake pedal stuck. When the gas pedal is stuck, you can't seem to stop revving. You have high anxiety and get easily angry. When the brake pedal is stuck, you can feel like you don't want to do anything at all. You will feel depressed and apathetic.

It is possible to have both the gas and the brake pedals stuck at the same time. When this happens, your body can feel like it wants to explode—feeling anxiety, anger, and despair at the same time puts incredible stress on your body.

Self-regulating refers to one's ability to recognize and control the impact of emotions on the body and the nervous system. Self-calming strategies like breathing and mindfulness can quiet a state of hyperarousal so the prefrontal cortex of the brain (the identity center) remains online. This allows people to act like themselves even during stressful situations. Once a person is able to self-regulate, they can start helping others. In technical terms, they become "external regulators," who help others learn to regulate their emotions so they don't stay overwhelmed or shut down.

Good parents routinely serve as "external regulators." They meet their child in the midst of their upset emotions and stay relationally engaged with them while they quiet. Because the parent is able to self-regulate, the child's nervous system can mirror the parent's nervous system. This first allows the child to co-regulate with the parent (quiet together) and then self-regulate (they learn how to quiet themselves by going through co-regulation again and again). The more often a child gets help quieting, the better their system will get at self-regulation.

Quieting exercises for the body

Given the direct relationship between the body and your emotions, it makes sense that quieting your emotions often starts with quieting your body. Here are a few exercises for you to practice. You can remember the first four with the word BEST. As in, these are the BEST practices for quieting your body.

» Breathe in a square.

» Exaggerate emotion.

» Sing and Soothe.

» Tense and Release.

Breathe in a square. One of the tools for controlling anxiety taught to Navy Seals is the practice of breathing in a square. You inhale (up). Hold (across). Exhale (down). Hold (across). As you breathe around the box (up, across, down, across) you do each step for four seconds. It is often helpful to repeat this process three or four times.

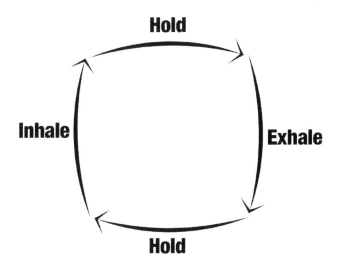

One of the reasons deep breathing is helpful is that, under stress, our breathing becomes very shallow and rapid. Controlling your breathing helps calm your body.

Exaggerate your emotion then relax. Have you ever noticed that it rarely does any good to tell someone who is agitated to calm down? Here are some exercises related to the two emotions that escalate our energy level.

1. <u>Fear</u>. When babies get scared, they have an involuntary reaction to throw their hands up and back. When you are feeling overwhelmed, find a private spot and try imitating this. Throw your hands up and back over your head while gasping like something has startled you. Then breathe deeply and slowly as you lower your hands to your waist. Repeat this three times. Jim Wilder teaches a form of this exercise that includes talking to yourself or singing to yourself as you slow your breathing. He suggests quoting Psalm 56:3, "When I am afraid, I will trust in you, O God."[6]

2. <u>Anger</u>. The Hebrew word for anger is the same word used for nose. This makes sense when you realize that anger tends to make your nostrils flare. To help quiet from anger, try flaring your nostrils, clenching your fists, and posing like a weightlifter or the Hulk. After tensing your muscles in this way, shake out your arms and rub them from top to bottom while you breathe deeply.

Sing and soothe. Singing helps both your right and left brain connect. If you can't think of anything else, just sing happy birthday to yourself. It is hard to do this and not smile and, of course, smiling is what we are after here!

Singing has been used to quiet emotions for centuries. David's music was used to soothe Saul's anger and anxiety.[7]

---

6 | See this demonstrated on YouTube at "Shalom Your Body" with Jim Wilder.
7 | 1 Samuel 16:23; 18:10; 19:9

Musical activities like whistling, humming, singing, or playing an instrument can distract and refocus our attention. It can be quieting or energizing. There is a reason singing babies to sleep is such a worldwide practice.

As a young mom with four children under the age of five, I (Stefanie) felt like I was living on the edge of my emotional capacity. I often felt alone, isolated, depressed, and anxious. One of the most powerful tools that I had was praise and worship. I would put whatever song was currently speaking to me on repeat, and I would will myself to sing along. As the truth from the song washed over me and I agreed with the words through singing, I would feel the heaviness start to lift. By the second or third repeat, I would find myself dancing in the kitchen with my kids, giggling and feeling joy together. These years taught me the power of praise. It can change the atmosphere in my soul and in my home.

Besides singing, some other ways to soothe your upset emotions involve changing your body chemistry.

1. Take a hot bath. Our hands get cold during an FFF reaction. This happens because the energy in our body goes to the core to prepare us for action. Warming up our hands (and the rest of us) sends the message that we can calm down. This is one of the reasons hot baths are so relaxing.

2. Snuggle up with a heavy, warm blanket.

3. Use candles, diffusers, baking, or other ways to create a pleasant aroma in the atmosphere.

Tense and release. Have you ever noticed that it is almost impossible to tell yourself to just relax? Instead, it helps to actually increase the tension in your body before you try to quiet it. One businessman who was angry and needed to calm down before he went into a meeting grabbed a towel from his desk, went into the bathroom, and twisted the towel really hard while blowing air out of his nose and making a grimacing face. He held his pose for about three seconds, breathed deeply then did it again. By the time he had done this twice, he felt his body relaxing and his emotions quieting.

» Tensing. A simple exercise for quieting your body is to tense and relax various muscle groups. Try this. Clench your fists and tighten your forearms for a count of five. Then loosen your fingers and flick them around for a count of five. Finish by rubbing your arms from top to bottom ten times and breathing deeply. Tightening and relaxing various muscle groups is helpful because it can be done practically anywhere, often discreetly.

» Yawning. Turning your head to the left and right and yawning deeply (in an exaggerated way) until you actually yawn is another good way to quiet your body. Yawning signals your body that it is time to quiet and rest.

» Exercising. Going for a run or doing some other kind of exercise to work off your adrenaline can help change your body chemistry and make it easier to quiet your body.

You can practice with a variety of different methods of quieting your body and find the ones that work best for you.

Quieting your mind

Quieting your body is helpful, but many times the issue is made worse by the fact that we cannot quiet our minds. Just as we used BEST to remember ways to quiet the body, we will use the word DREAM to remember ways of quieting the mind.

» Distract yourself.

» Replace your thoughts.

» Engage relationally.

» Appreciate for five minutes.

» Make a plan.

1. **Distract yourself.** It is virtually impossible to tell yourself not to think about something. In fact, the more you try not to think about something, the more you think about it. A better strategy is to distract yourself with something else. One of the challenges with this is, if I am anxious, it is hard to believe anything other than my problems deserve any of my attention.

Distraction is basically doing something that requires your focus. For example, sometimes it is helpful to get busy with work. It can be helpful to start doing tasks. Often these tasks require enough focus that you soon find yourself distracted from what you had been thinking about. This gives your mind a chance to break the cycle of anxious thinking through distraction. Many times when I was feeling anxious, I started answering emails, worked on a project around the house, or got busy with some other task only to realize half an hour later that my anxiety had quieted.

2. **Replace your thoughts.** Most of us try to resolve our anxious thinking by constant problem solving. This rarely works because there is no end to the problems we can imagine. It is better to focus on something else.

The temptation when you feel anxious is to reason with yourself about why it is foolish to be anxious. However, the very process of trying to think it through keeps you focused on what is producing the anxiety. Here are two examples of replacing your thoughts. The first is a form of distraction. You simply start thinking about something else and soon you stop thinking about what had your mind racing. For instance, I (Marcus) will often start thinking about memories from my childhood that involve riding my bike or playing baseball. Other times I will revisit a favorite movie or book and focus on the story. In some ways, it doesn't matter what you think about as long as it isn't the anxiety-producing thought. The goal is to break the hold the anxious thoughts have on you.

The second example involves prayer. You can ask God to show you how the devil is trying to get you to think about your situation. It usually produces shame, fear, anger, or some other negative emotion. Then ask God to give you a different way to think about the situation or a different picture of what is going on.

When Brenda and I lived in Texas, I remember one night I got very angry with her (I don't remember why). I got in the car and drove to the grocery store. As I went, I focused on all the reasons why I was justified in feeling upset. In the middle of this, however, I had a God-thought. "Marcus, you are just being selfish." The thought wasn't an angry one. It was corrective. I actually had to laugh. It felt like a dad telling a little boy to look at a situation from a different perspective. Relatively quickly, I was able to change my attitude because God had given me a new outlook. Brenda and I ended up having a very enjoyable evening together.

3. **Engage relationally.** Engaging in a relational conversation can often help your right brain get back online and minimize your sense of overwhelm. Genuine curiosity in someone else and appreciation for them can help take the focus off of your problems. On one long road trip when I (Marcus) was by myself and battling some anxiety, I called

a number of friends just to have conversations that kept my mind occupied and built a sense of connection that both distracted and helped get my relational circuits back online. I often find that getting your relational circuits re-engaged helps your body calm more quickly.

4.   **Appreciate for five minutes.** As noted already, sometimes appreciation can help you quiet. At other times you need to quiet before you can appreciate. A great way to focus your thoughts is to come up with a Top Ten list of things you appreciate. Appreciation can help distract you from your anxious thoughts and replace those thoughts with a focus on what you enjoy in life. If you need help focusing, journal your appreciation. You can do this with a pen and paper or on your computer. You may not feel joy immediately, but the task of writing out what you appreciate is helpful. Sharing what you have written with someone else often helps get your relational circuits back online, too.

5.   **Make a plan.** If you have a plan, you have hope. Faith is trusting that God has a plan and that His plan is good even if I don't know what it is. This strategy has four steps.

» Ask yourself, "What is the worst thing that could happen?" Write it out.

» Ask yourself, "What is the best thing that could happen?" Write that out.

» Ask yourself, "What is the most likely thing to happen?" Write that out.

» Now make a plan based on what you think is the most likely thing to happen.

We just went through an exercise like this at a church board meeting. COVID-19 had been international news for several weeks, and the first case had just been reported in our state. We had a meeting and went through this four-step process (though we didn't write out our answers). We discussed various scenarios, then made a plan on what we would actually do in terms of preparation and communication.

A JOY WORKOUT

Quieting is a crucial life skill. Some studies suggest that nothing does more to determine your long-term emotional health than developing the ability to quiet yourself after your emotions get upset. Taken together, quieting and appreciation make for a great joy workout.

In this chapter we have focused on ways to help you quiet your body and your thoughts. You learned BEST (Breathe, Exaggerate, Sing, Tense) for quieting your body, and DREAM (distract, replace, engage, appreciate, make a plan) for quieting your mind.

Appreciation and quieting often work together to help us regulate our emotions. Here is an exercise to try.

1. Stand up and shrug your shoulders then let them fall while letting out a big breath.

2. Keeping your head still, move your eyes to the left for a count of three, then move them to the right for a count of three, then look up for a count of three, then down for a count of three. Repeat this two or three times.

3. Hold your hands above your head and squeeze them into fists. Hold your grip firm for five seconds, then shake out your arms and rub them from your elbow to your wrist a few times. Repeat this three times.

4. Breathe in a square three times (See page 73).

5. Rub your arms from shoulder to elbow ten times while breathing normally.

6. Sit down and think about a favorite activity. For example, I (Marcus) often picture myself hitting a baseball and relive the feeling of the crack of the ball off the bat. Sometimes I do this with tennis or golf, too. You might recall the feeling you had playing an instrument or swimming or riding a bike or creating art. Whatever it is, let your mind dwell on it for two minutes.

7. Close your eyes. Breathe normally. Rest.

LOOKING AHEAD

Now that we have explored the importance of quieting and learned some practical ways to build it into our lives, it is time to learn about one of the most powerful joy producers in the world—appreciation. Together, quieting and appreciation form a powerful one-two punch for building joy.

CHAPTER FIVE
appreciation

There is a difference between left brain appreciation and right brain appreciation. Left brain appreciation notices that the sunset is pretty. You may even comment on it or take a picture of it on your phone. Right brain appreciation sits on a rock or a park bench and watches the sunset for five minutes and drinks in the experience. It engages with the feelings that are stirring inside, smells the aroma in the air, feels the cool breeze, soaks up the experience. Later, it revisits that experience as it shares the feelings and sensations with others. Right brain appreciation engages all of our senses and shares the joy with others.

For Christians, appreciation goes beyond a brain exercise. It is an act of connection with God. As we take the time to feel appreciation, we direct our attention to God and invite Him to meet us in that moment. Sometimes this act of worship focuses directly on who God is and what He has done. At other times, we simply acknowledge that "every good and every perfect gift is from above" (James 1:17).

The apostle Paul routinely encourages his readers to practice appreciation.[1] This is especially significant because Paul suffered a great deal. He was imprisoned, whipped, stoned, ridiculed, chased, shipwrecked, and more. Yet, Paul does not seem to have been traumatized by all of his suffer-

---

1 | Colossians 3:15, "Let the peace of Christ rule in your hearts . . . and be thankful." Colossians 4:2, "Devote yourselves to prayer, being watchful and thankful." We also find this in Hebrews 12:28, "let us be thankful, and so worship God acceptably with reverence and awe."

ing. One of his secrets was the practice of appreciation as a means of directly connecting with God. We see a vivid example of this when he and his companion Silas were wrongly arrested, beaten, and thrown into a foreign prison. How did he spend that evening? Singing songs of praise and thanks to God! I find that remarkable.

> BUILD HABITS WHILE YOU HAVE THE CAPACITY TO WORK ON THEM.

It is difficult to build a habit while you are in distress. It is much better to build habits while you have the capacity to work on them. It is a good idea to start small and build up to bigger and bigger issues. Sometimes the gap between where we are and where we want to be feels so big that we vacillate between trying to fix everything at once and doing nothing. It can be helpful to work on one habit at a time. Building time into your daily calendar to do quieting and appreciation exercises for 30 days or more is a great way to start.

When I (Marcus) first tried this, I thought it was impossible. I could hardly smile, let alone stay in a state of appreciation for five minutes. The very attempt to do this exercise increased my negative emotions because I couldn't do it! If you struggle like this, it might help to do these exercises with one or two other people. Sometimes engaging relationally with others helps us get past the feeling of being stuck. With this in mind, it is often necessary to practice quieting before diving into appreciation.

In the last chapter, we discussed quieting and building rhythm. In this chapter we focus on building joy through appreciation. One reason appreciation is so effective in growing joy is that it combines beliefs and connections (the B and C of ABC). When you practice appreciation, you are setting your mind (beliefs) on what there is to enjoy and sharing that experience with God and/or others (connections).

GAMES

There is a lot in life to appreciate, but sometimes we need help getting them in focus. To help with this we often use the acrostic GAMES.

- » **Gratitude**
- » **Anticipation**
- » **Memories**
- » **Experiences**
- » **Singing**

The first three practices represent the present, the future, and the past. *Gratitude* is appreciating what is happening in the present. *Anticipation* is appreciating what you are looking forward to in the future. *Memories* is reflecting on what you appreciate from the past.

The final two practices refer to activities you can generate. *Experiences* refers to creating an experience that is designed to share joy. *Singing*, of course, is a great activity for generating joy through appreciation.

Gratitude. For our purposes, gratitude relates to what we have to appreciate in the present. For example, I (Marcus) am at a coffee shop with my daughter on a beautiful summer day. There are gorgeous flowers in full bloom just outside the window. I am enjoying a way-too-sweet latte (the whipped cream was awesome!). As I write this, it gives me a chance to enjoy my surroundings and live in the moment with gratitude. Far too often, I am in places like this getting work done without taking the time to drink in the atmosphere and enjoy the moment.

Learning how to let yourself enter into the feeling of gratitude for five minutes or more helps your body relax and your mind quiet. What is there in the present that makes you smile? This could be food. Do you like mangos, or coffee, or coffee cake? It could be nature. Do you like the clouds or the water or the trees? It could be people you are with or decorations you see. It really doesn't matter. The idea is to notice something in the moment that you enjoy, then dwell on that feeling.

When Paul and Silas were in prison, they quieted themselves and returned to joy by singing praise songs and expressing gratitude to God for His eternal blessings. Gratitude for what is eternal and spiritual is another excellent way to practice appreciation for what is happening in the present.

Anticipation. If gratitude is appreciation for the present, anticipation is appreciation for what you are looking forward to in the future. In my case, I am not only at a nice coffee shop with my daughter, but I also know that my wife is on her way here. I am looking forward to seeing her and sharing her joy because I know how much she loves this place and how much she loves being with us. I'm sure we will take a walk and look at the flowers and possibly get dinner together later.

I once heard someone say, "Never surprise your wife with a European vacation—because I know all of you men out there are planning to do that!" He went on to make the point that the anticipation of such a vacation is half the fun. Sometimes it's more fun than the actual experience. While most of us probably don't have major events like a European vacation looming on the horizon, it is always a great idea to have little things to look forward to and to give ourselves permission to dwell on the joy they can bring.

Is there anything in the future that you are looking forward to? This doesn't have to be life-changing, just something enjoyable. Do you have plans to spend time with anyone this week? Do you have a favorite TV show coming on soon? Are you looking forward to getting something done or taking a nap? Taking a few minutes to think about something you are looking forward to is a good way to practice appreciation.

Memories. Reliving joy from the past is a great form of appreciation. This is a huge category. Some of you have a lot of trauma in your past, and it is easy to think that the past has nothing joyful in it. However, if you give it a little thought, something has probably made you smile. We recommend making Top Five or Top Ten lists of your favorite memories. Here are some categories to consider.

» **Childhood memories:**

> » Favorite TV shows
>
> » Favorite vacation memories
>
> » Favorite holiday memories
>
> » Favorite hobbies or sports memories
>
> » Favorite creative ideas

> Examples: Stefanie has photo albums from different seasons in her childhood that contain memories. Marcus has a collection of baseballs from Little League and junior baseball. Each one memorializes a great game. They evoke good emotions every time he sees them. Marcus's wife, Brenda, keeps files of pictures from childhood on her phone so that she can review them and spend time remembering.

» **Young Adult memories:**

> » Friends from high school or college
>
> » Events that made you smile
>
> » Creative things you did with friends
>
> » Favorite movies from your college years

> Examples: Marcus likes to close his eyes and take mental walks around the various campuses where he attended school and remember the people he would see there.

» **Family memories (if you are a parent):**
   » Courtship memories
   » Wedding memories
   » Family holidays
   » Family vacations

Examples: Both Marcus and Stefanie have pictures of family around the house. Wedding photos. Happy moments with the kids. It isn't always pictures. It can be souvenirs, too.

» **Nature memories:**
   » Mountains
   » Water
   » Snow
   » Memorable weather events

Examples: Marcus and Brenda decorate the house with a nature theme. Brenda keeps calendars of National Parks around to evoke the joy of nature and the nostalgia of happy family vacations. Marcus has an Ansel Adams picture of El Capitan rising through the clouds on a crisp winter day hanging over his desk. Stefanie and her family take a "stone of remembrance" from everywhere they travel and store them in a decorative way in the house. Sometimes it is an actual stone that gets added to a jar of sand but often it is a picture book of the state park or landscape. This serves as a reminder of the trip and is also a way to continue to appreciate and enjoy the nature.

As you can see, there is almost no end to the possibilities when it comes to collecting joyful memories. It can be helpful to collect these in places where you can look at pictures and reminisce. We used to do this with scrapbooks, but now they tend to get collected on cell phones and computers. Decide what would be most accessible and life-giving to you.

Experiences. If the first three practices have to do with the present, the future, and the past, this one has to do with being creative. The idea here is to plan an event or activity you would enjoy. Plan a vacation. Design a house. Invite some friends to get together. Is there an experience you can plan that would be fun to think about? Even if you don't follow through with the experience, sometimes it can be fun just to plan it.

I (Stefanie) like to decorate with pictures and memories that bring me joy. I have a favorite place. It is a cove in a lake that my family has enjoyed for over a decade. That one place represents more than fifteen years of joy for me. It is a place where my family has played together, laughed together, and enjoyed the warmth of the sunshine on our skin. We even have a playlist of our favorite "lake songs." Two years ago, I decided to take a picture of one of my favorite scenes on the lake so I could capture the beauty of the place. I had the picture enlarged, got it framed, and put it on my mantle. Now, every day as I go about my business, I get to look at the calm, blue green water, tall bluffs, majestic trees, and beautiful blue sky. The picture triggers something in my brain to remember the joy of the times spent there.

This year I made it my goal to make a painting of the picture. I spend a few minutes each day working on this home-made piece of art. This gives me time each day to enjoy and appreciate this special place and all that it means to me.

Singing. There is truth in the adage, "Whistle while you work." Singing, humming, and whistling can help you transition into a place of appreciation. It can help to make a list of favorite songs that make you smile. As we have seen, the apostle Paul was certainly a big believer in singing, as he wrote to the Colossians, "Let the message of Christ dwell among you richly as you teach and admonish one another with all wisdom through psalms, hymns, and songs from the Spirit, singing to God with gratitude in your hearts" (3:16).

Music is a great way to evoke appreciation. Sometimes music comes with memories. So, it can be a great way to bring up emotions from the past you want to relive: favorite movie scores, happy party music, meaningful spiritual songs, and songs that just make you smile.

Examples: Recently I (Marcus) spent time watching You-Tube videos of some of my favorite bands from high school. I was surprised at how many emotions the music stirred and how much fun it was. Music can take you back to an earlier time in life and lots of memories that make you smile. Additionally, just the act of singing brings the left and right hemispheres of the brain together in a way that little else can.

APPRECIATING GOD

While all appreciation is a form of worship, it is also helpful to set aside time to reflect specifically on the attributes and actions of God. Here are a few tools you might consider as you start this process.

1. Names. Begin collecting a list of the names of God and ordering them from A to Z.

2. Attributes. Paul wrote that God's invisible qualities are clearly seen from what has been created (Romans 1:20). Take time to list and meditate on those qualities.

3. Provisions. Collect stories of times when you were in need and God provided for your needs.

4. Promises. Collect promises from the Bible and write about ways God has fulfilled those promises in your life.

5. <u>Abundance</u>. Reflect on times of abundance, when God provided far more than you needed.

6. <u>Spiritual Blessings</u>. Paul wrote that God has given us "every spiritual blessing in Christ" (Ephesians 1:3). Begin making a list of those blessings starting with your identity in Christ and the inheritance you have in heaven.

Categories like these can be helpful in jumpstarting appreciation toward God. It can also be helpful to collect a variety of practices that give you focus. Here are a few samples.

1. Gratitude journal

2. Letters to God

3. Creating art (music, poetry, painting, etc.)

One way to practice appreciation as worship collectively is by building appreciation altars. For example, in my book *The Deeper Walk Guide to Advent* I (Marcus) encourage families to have everyone place a small stone in the middle of the table as they go around and each express some reason for thanks. As stones collect, they become an altar of appreciation that can expand throughout the holiday season. I have done something similar at marriage retreats. We give rocks and a permanent marker to each couple. They take a moment to reflect on what they have to appreciate and write something on the rock to represent their appreciation. We then go into a field and add those rocks to others that have been placed there. The result is a growing "altar of appreciation" that expands with each new group.

A JOY WORKOUT

Building the habits of quieting and appreciation will grow your emotional capacity in the same way that working out will grow your physical capacity. Establishing a routine built around appreciation will train your brain to search for what there is to enjoy in life and help you learn to live with gratitude.

Several years ago, I (Marcus) spoke at a retreat for missionaries who had just returned from the field. One of them was so joyful and filled with such obvious "bounce" I asked her if she had a secret to her contagious attitude. She laughed and said, "I wasn't always this way. My first year on the mission field I was almost sent home for my critical attitude." She told me how she complained about everything—the weather, the food, the accommodations, even the people she had come to help. She was basically told to shape up or ship out. Her transformation started when she began a gratitude journal. She spent about half an hour every day journaling about what she had to be grateful for. Twenty years later, she was a model of joyful living.

Appreciation Journal

To start your own joy workout program, it can be helpful to do what this missionary did and start an appreciation journal. Take ten to twenty minutes to write out what you have to be grateful for today. Re-read your journaling from time to time and occasionally read it to others.

My now-departed step-mother (Eileen Lageer Warner) showed me a stack of gratitude journals she had been keeping for over twenty-five years. Every day, she took time to write about what she had to appreciate in life, and it showed in her upbeat and sparkling personality.

CHAPTER SIX
beliefs

The world is filled with stories about the power of beliefs. Some beliefs are limiting. Some are empowering. When your thinking gets off, it can affect every area of your life. I (Marcus) learned this lesson very vividly when I played Little League baseball. I was normally a very good batter and led my team in both home runs and batting average. During one season, however, I went into a slump. I just stopped hitting well.

At the time, my dad was listening to some tapes by a sports psychologist who was teaching about the power of visualization in sports. As an experiment, my dad asked me to sit in a chair, close my eyes and picture myself hitting a baseball. To my utter amazement, I could not do it. Something went wrong every time—I would have a hitch in my swing, foul the ball off, miss the ball altogether. I literally could not picture myself hitting the ball properly.

So, my dad took another step. We went to a field with a bucket of baseballs. He pitched them to me but told me not to swing until I had pictured myself hitting the ball perfectly three times in a row. After about ten or twelve pitches, something clicked and suddenly I couldn't imagine NOT hitting the baseball. I swung at the next four pitches and hit four straight home runs.

The confidence stayed with me. When I closed my eyes and pictured myself hitting, the ball felt so large and slow that I couldn't miss it. The next game I hit home runs in my first two at bats. I hit a double on my third at bat simply because I was so impatient I literally hit a ball that had bounced in the dirt on the way to the plate. I still hit it hard because it felt impossible not to hit a baseball solidly.

That experience made a big impression on me as I realized how powerful our beliefs are and how important it is to get the picture in our mind right. This is especially true of the way we see God and the way we see ourselves, but it is also true of the way we see all sorts of people and situations.

In several marriage retreats I helped to run, we gave the couples a simple exercise. Close your eyes and think about your husband or your wife. What do you see? It was amazing how many people couldn't picture the other person as happy to be with them. We took it a step further and asked, "How does the devil want you to see your spouse?" In almost every case, people saw someone who was scary, unjust, disgusting, or in some other way defective. A big part of the weekend for many of the people was beginning to picture their partner as someone loveable.

FIVE ENGINES

When it comes to understanding emotions there are five engines that can play a role.

1. **Our body.** If there is something physically wrong with you, it can play a huge role in the way you feel. From lack of sleep to tumors in the brain, from chemical reactions to schizophrenic disorders, your body can have a profound impact on your emotions. This is why sleep, exercise, proper diet, hormonal supplements, and the right medications can have a big impact on how we feel.

2. **Our beliefs.** Beliefs are related to the narrative engine on the left side of the brain. What you believe about people and situations will drive the way you

feel about them. Getting our beliefs sorted out is an important part of regulating our emotions.

3. **Our bonding.** Bonding is related to the relational engine on the right side of the brain. There are essentially two types of bonds that people can form—joy bonds and fear bonds. When I am joy-bonded to someone, I can feel joy just thinking about them. But when I am fear-bonded to someone, I can start to feel anxiety anticipating our next connection. The type of bond you have with someone can have a profound impact on how you feel. It is much easier to believe negative things about people when we are bonded to them in fear.

Beyond these physical engines, there are two spiritual engines that can impact our emotions.

4. **The Holy Spirit.** The Holy Spirit can affect all three of our physical "emotion engines." He can affect our body, our beliefs, and our bonding. He can heal. He can reveal truth, and walking in the Spirit produces love, joy, and peace—profoundly good emotional and relational fruit.

5. **Wicked Spirits.** Spirits from the kingdom of darkness can also affect all three of our "emotion engines." They are deceiving spirits, so their lies can imprison us. They are dividing spirits who generate factions, envy, strife, and other "fear bonding" activities. They can also affect the body. Many of the physical healings recorded in the Bible were accomplished by the casting out of a demon.

With these engines in mind, we understand that all of them play a role in building bounce. We want to get free and stay free of demonic activity. We want to walk in the Spirit on all occasions. We want to glorify God in our bodies. We want to love others and, as we will focus on here, we want to renew our minds and take every thought captive.

Beliefs and emotions are closely entwined. Sometimes emotions follow beliefs. For example, if I think you lied about me, that belief will affect my emotions. Or, if I think you are about to give me a thousand dollars, that belief will also affect my emotions. On the other hand, sometimes beliefs follow emotions. For example, when you feel shame, it is easier to believe thoughts that support shame. Once you feel shame, it is easier to believe shaming thoughts. If you feel shame about one issue, it is easy to remember all of the other times you felt like a bad person. The way you are feeling drives the direction your thoughts take. I (Marcus) experience this a lot in my marriage. When I am upset with Brenda, it is easier to believe negative things about her. When I am attracted to Brenda, it is harder to think negative thoughts about her. Keeping our relationship good makes it easier to keep my thoughts good.

THE POWER OF NARRATIVE

The left side of your brain can be thought of as your narrative engine. Part of its job is to explain life. It is constantly trying to anticipate the future by learning from the past. Narratives teach your brain what is important and what can be ignored. Sadly, the narratives we create are often wrong.

For example, if you have a narrative about one of your children that says, "This is the good kid," and a narrative about another child that says, "This kid is trouble," your brain learns to look for evidence that supports the narrative. It also learns to suppress evidence that contradicts the narrative. We see this principle at work in politics and the media on a regular basis. Once you believe a narrative, it can blind you to evidence that contradicts the storyline. At the same time, it amplifies evidence that supports the narrative. Here are a few examples.

1. The power of narrative is a powerful element of propaganda. When America entered the Great War (WWI), polls showed the country was split almost 50/50 as to which side to support. There was a lot of empathy for the Germans. So, by executive order, President Woodrow Wilson created a new propaganda agency and put his campaign manager, George Creel, in charge of it.[1] This new federal agency was given the task of raising support for the war against Germany. It was so successful in demonizing the Germans and raising support for the British that in less than two years the polls showed that 90% of Americans favored war against Germany. The war was cast as a fight between civilization (The British Commonwealth) and barbarianism (The Huns). It was touted as a war to make the world safe for democracy. Yet, it could be argued that the war did the opposite and paved the way for the most terrible totalitarian states in history—Franco, Mussolini, Hitler, Stalin, and Mao.

   The stories of propaganda swaying the beliefs of a culture can be multiplied many times over. Just as propaganda has a powerful influence in politics, so your brain's narrative engine is like its very own propaganda department. If it can control what you believe, your beliefs will control how you feel, and how you feel has a tremendous impact on how you behave.

2. The power of narrative can have an enormous impact on relationships. If you believe lies about someone, your emotions will react to what you believe even if it isn't true. A great example of this can be seen in Jane

---

1 | "How Woodrow Wilson's Propaganda Machine Changed American Journalism" at Smithsonianmag.com.

Austen's beloved novel *Pride and Prejudice*. In this romantic tale, Lizzy at first believes that Mr. Darcy is conceited and contemptable. She loathes him and adores his friend, Mr. Wickham. By the end of the story, the truth has been revealed that Mr. Wickham is the contemptable man, and Lizzy falls in love with the honorable and dependable Mr. Darcy.

3. The power of narrative can limit or unleash our potential. A limiting belief is one that creates a mental barrier. For example, before the 1950s it was believed by many in the scientific community that it was impossible for a human to run a mile in under four minutes. Some doctors predicted running that fast would cause a person's lungs to explode. Today, it is common for elite athletes to run a mile in under four minutes. But, before that could happen, the mental barrier saying it was impossible had to be broken. Thus, when Rodger Bannister broke the barrier for the first time on May 6th, 1954, it was considered a miracle.

One of the reasons the Bible speaks so often about meditation on God's Word and renewing the mind is that these practices activate our brain's natural tendency to amplify what we think is important.

There is virtually no end to stories illustrating the power of narrative. What you believe about yourself, God, and other people will drive the way you feel about them.

THE BATTLE FOR THE MIND

The essence of spiritual warfare is a battle for the mind. Jesus said the devil is a murderer and the father of lies (John 8:44). This means all deception has its roots in satanic activity and has the goal of creating death and destruction. Satan uses deception to create slavery that ends in death. The purpose of Satan's lies is to ensnare us. Deception is like the carrot that lures the rabbit into the trap. The carrot tempts the rabbit. The carrot comes with an inherent promise of something good (life-giving, tasty food!), when it is actually there to lure the rabbit into evil (slavery and death).

DECEPTIVE THINKING IS OFTEN MISLEADING BECAUSE THE THOUGHTS IN OUR HEAD ARE TRUE.

Deception works just like an illusion done by a magician. The illusionist allows you to see several elements of his performance that are true, but he hides elements that would take away the illusion that magic had happened. As long as you only think about the true elements of the routine you can see, you will never know the truth. In the same way, deceptive thinking is often misleading because the thoughts in our head are true. It's just that other true thoughts that would change the picture are missing. For example, have you ever had someone wave at you, causing you to smile and wave back, only to realize they were interacting with someone else? What you saw was true. They were looking your way. They were waving like they wanted engagement. But another true element was missing that changed everything—they were looking past you at someone else.

When it comes to the way we see God or ourselves, we sometimes miss the fact that we are deceived because we have true memories or true thoughts in our mind. We are just missing other true thoughts that would completely change the picture. For example, I know people who hated God because He did not stop some great tragedy from occurring. It was true that God had allowed the tragedy. As long as they focused only on that truth, they could think of no justification for God and believed Him to be unworthy of their trust. However, many of these same people have encountered Jesus during prayer for inner healing and completely changed their minds about God because they learned there was more to the story than they had imagined.

One startling example of this came from a woman who had survived ritual torture. During the experience, another child had died. In that moment, the surviving girl believed the lie that God was unfair because he had allowed the other girl to escape the suffering (through death), but had left her there to endure it. Years later, she met Jesus in that memory and saw that God had provided for both girls. The girl who died was taken to heaven, but the girl who lived had also been provided for. God had sent a giant angel to watch over her and had already put a journey together that would lead her to healing and redemption.

When we believe the devil's lies, we enter into an agreement with him. This agreement says, "You are right, and God is wrong." Such an agreement gives him permission to a place in our lives from which to exert influence and control (Ephesians 4:26-27). This is why Jesus says, "The truth will set you free" (John 8:32). It is also why the Bible places such an importance on winning the battle for our minds by filling them with what is true.

» Proverbs warns us to guard our hearts (Proverbs 4:23).

» Jesus calls us to repent—a word that literally means to change the way we think about life.

» Paul urges Christians to renew their minds (Romans 12:2) and to take thoughts captive (2 Corinthians 10:5).

» Paul encourages us to set our minds on what is true, noble, right, pure, lovely, admirable, excellent, and praiseworthy (Philippians 4:8).

The very shape of the Hebrew Bible is a call to biblical meditation. The Hebrew Scriptures are divided into three sections: the Torah, the Prophets, and the Writings. In the first chapter of the first book of the Prophets we read, "Meditate on the Torah day and night" (Joshua 1:8). In the first chapter of the first book of the Writings we read, "Meditate on the Torah" (Psalm 1:2). Meditation on Torah is held out as the key to obedience and a deep connection with God that bears fruit.

The priority God places on winning the battle for your mind by keeping His Word constantly on our thoughts and on our lips is hard to miss.

MEANING MAKERS

We are meaning makers. We are wired to take in data from our world (make observations), find the meaning of the data (interpret it), and draw conclusions based on our interpretations (apply it). Over time, these conclusions become generalized and develop into a lens through which we interpret life's experiences. The problem is that many of us have drawn our conclusions based on faulty interpretations because of poorly formed lenses.

One of the reasons lenses get warped is that our narrative engines don't get enough information. When we get triggered and our FFF response takes over, the right side of our brain can send very incomplete information to the left side. This means the more overwhelmed we are, the less likely it is that we are going to form a correct interpretation of what is going on.

A common ploy of fiction writers is to have one or more of their characters offer an interpretation of the evidence that has been introduced to the reader. Take a murder mystery for instance. In most murder mysteries, several characters will suggest possible explanations for the clues provided. Rarely do any of them have it right, though each of their stories assembles the evidence in a coherent way. In the same way, your brain naturally creates a narrative based on the evidence it has at its disposal. Rarely is that narrative totally accurate, and sometimes it can be wildly off the mark.

When Proverbs says, "Trust in the LORD with all your heart and lean not on your own understanding," it is giving us a path through all of the uncertainty.[2] It is very easy for our beliefs to lead to a wrong understanding of life. So, God makes it easy for us. He says, "Don't try to figure it all out. Trust me."

THE LENS WE USE WILL INFORM US IF WE ARE LIVING IN A STORY OF DOOM OR A STORY OF REDEMPTION.

I (Stefanie) have learned a profound truth from years of work as a Christian counselor. Experience is more powerful than words. I can tell someone that God loves them, that God has never left them or abandoned them. If their evidence tells a different story, however, they will look at me and say, "I want to believe that. I know that's the correct Sunday school answer, but my evidence is screaming that it's a lie."

There are really only two lenses by which we can interpret the world around us: Fear and Love. The lens we use will inform us if we are living in a story of doom or a story of redemption. I would love to say that we always have a choice which lens we adopt, but the truth is, if we are stuck on one of the lower levels of the joy elevator, we cannot always make that choice.

After my own healing journey and 20 years of walking with people through the healing process, there is one thing I know for sure. Jesus is able to guide people out of the dark prison of fear and into the light of His redemptive love, changing their narrative forever. I have seen clients invite Jesus into the most painful places of their story, the very

2 | Proverbs 3:5

places where belief systems were most broken and—in many cases—the place where their faulty belief system was born. In every case, Jesus spoke truth to their heart and met them in an experiential way that melted away their belief in the devil's lies. Because of the work Jesus did, their false beliefs were replaced with truth.

Principle 1: Beliefs drive emotions.

In his best-selling book *Victory Over the Darkness*, Neil T. Anderson emphasizes the role of beliefs in driving emotions. These beliefs are often rooted in goals we feel we must attain in order to be successful. When our beliefs about what it means to be a success are out of line with God's, it triggers the warning signs of negative emotions such as anger, anxiety, and depression.

> » **Anger.** "When your activity in a relationship or a project results in feelings of anger, it is usually because someone or something has blocked your goal, something or somebody is preventing you from accomplishing what you wanted."[3]

> » **Anxiety.** "When you feel anxious in a task or a relationship, your anxiety may be signaling that your goal may be uncertain. You are hoping something will happen, but you have no guarantee it will. You can control some of the factors but not all of them."[4]

> » **Depression.** "When you base your future success on something that can never happen, you have a hopeless impossible goal. Your depression is a signal that your goal, no matter how spiritual or how noble, may never be reached."[5]

---

3 | Neil T. Anderson, *Victory Over the Darkness* (Minneapolis: Bethany House, 2000, 2013) p. 126.

4 | *Victory Over the Darkness*, p. 127.

5 | *Victory Over the Darkness*, p. 127.

Dr. Anderson suggests that we need to change our beliefs in order to change these emotions.

Not all emotions are driven by beliefs. Many emotions—and often our deepest emotions—have to do with experiences that are much deeper than what we believe. Attachment pain, for instance, is not simply driven by beliefs. It is driven by a deep, God-given longing/need for secure, calm connections. The point is not that all emotions are driven by beliefs, but that our beliefs can drive emotions in some very profound ways.

Principle 2: Emotions can't distinguish a true belief from a false one.

Emotions can change very quickly when our beliefs change. When I (Marcus) was in junior high, I was playing upstairs in my house with some friends when I noticed a shadowy figure walk by the second-floor window. I whispered to my friends, "Hey, I just saw someone walking on the roof." Immediately, we ran downstairs. When we got to the kitchen, I saw a brown car I had never seen before parked in the driveway. At this point, I was feeling a high level of adventure. I wasn't scared so much as I felt like I was solving a crime.

Feeling much unwarranted confidence, I grabbed a baseball bat and went outside. As I walked around to the side of the house where I had seen the man on the roof, I looked, and he was still there! My emotions changed instantly, however, when I realized it was my older brother. His friend in the brown car was dropping him off, but he was locked out of the house and looking for a way in. I had not heard him knocking on the door, so he had climbed up on the roof and was hoping to find an open window to climb through. Nothing was the way I had imagined it to be. As long as I believed a burglar was trying to break into the house, my emotions were driven by that belief. As soon as my beliefs changed, my emotions changed, too.

Because beliefs are so important to emotions and emotions are so important to the choices we make, whoever can control what you believe can control how you feel and how you behave. This is why media is so important and why control of the narrative is so important in politics. The power of beliefs to sway behavior is also an issue that lies at the heart of spiritual warfare. The devil is called the father of lies, because he is an expert at influencing our beliefs, so we do what pleases him rather than what pleases God. In all of these settings, whoever controls your narrative, controls your emotions and can drive the way you live.

The biblical story of Elijah revolves around a battle over whose narrative was true. Elijah declared that there would be no rain except at his word for the next several years.[6] This was a direct attack on Baal, who was—among other things—the god of storms. Most ancient images of Baal show him holding a lightning bolt, which would imply that he was pretty good at hurling fire from the sky as well as sending rain.

The narrative seems pretty straight forward. Yahweh, the God of Israel, was declaring war on Baal and proving His power over him. However, the text makes it clear that almost no one believed this narrative. Elijah was seen as the bad guy. King Ahab calls him "the troubler of Israel."[7] The narrative preached by Ahab and Jezebel was not that Yahweh was greater than Baal, but that Baal had been offended. They believed Elijah had insulted their god, and now the storm god was not sending rain until they found the prophet and killed him. Those are pretty different narratives.

If you believe Elijah's narrative, the proper response is repentance. If you believe the narrative spun by Ahab and

6 | 1 Kings 17:1

7 | 1 Kings 18:17

Jezebel, the proper response is to hate Elijah. Talk about a culture war! The issue could only be resolved by a direct confrontation between Yahweh and Baal. This is why the two sides met at Mount Carmel. They wanted to see whose narrative was actually true, and whose was a lie.

Mount Carmel was home to an important temple to Baal. As the highest point in the area, it had been dedicated to the god whose storms swept in from the Mediterranean and brought the rains needed for the crops to grow. However, Mount Carmel was also claimed by Yahweh. According to the Hebrew Scriptures, the whole earth belongs to Yahweh,[8] and Mount Carmel in particular was part of the chosen land Yahweh had given to His people.[9] It was a good location for the contest. It was also a fair fight. Baal was supposed to be really good at sending rain and lightning, so striking an altar with fire from the sky should have been easy for him.

As you probably already know, however, Yahweh won this contest in a truly decisive fashion. Even though the priests and prophets of Baal numbered in the hundreds, and even though they had all day to offer sacrifices in a place that was sacred to Baal, nothing happened. Then Elijah built a simple stone altar, dug a trench around it and had it saturated with water until the trench was full. He did all of this just to make it clear that there was no trickery involved. If his God answered with fire it wouldn't happen because Elijah had cheated. In the end, none of this really mattered. Out of a clear blue sky, Yahweh sent such an enormous ball of fire that the entire altar was consumed.[10] No one could misunderstand what had happened. Elijah had proven that his narrative was correct. Yahweh was the true God who had held back the rain and exposed Baal as an imposter.

8 | Psalm 24:1

9 | Genesis 15:18

10 | We know it was a clear, blue sky because after the contest Elijah prayed seven times before a single cloud appeared on the horizon (1 Kings 18:38).

What is truly remarkable about this story is that Baal worship never died out in Israel. In fact, within a few generations, the worship of Baal was as prevalent as ever.[11] There are two important reasons lies hold on in cultures (and individuals). One reason is that there is a real devil who is actively working to keep his lies alive. People who have come under the influence of the enemy can be hardened and blinded so they simply can't see truth anymore.

Another reason lies can hold on is that following the truth might force us to break with our people. If you stop believing what your family or your friends believe, there can be dire consequences. I have a friend who grew up in India, and when he announced to his father that he had become a Christian, his father pulled out a knife and tried to kill him. Even if your situation is not that extreme, going against what your friends and family want you to believe and want you to value can be very hard.

Principle 3: Attachments influence beliefs and also drive emotions.

We want to be careful not to imply that beliefs are the only force driving emotions. In emphasizing the important role beliefs play, we don't want to miss out on the fact that at an even deeper level of brain function, emotions and behavior are driven by attachment.

Who you love has incredible influence over what you believe and how you behave. If the people you love are all conservative Republicans, it is easy to love conservatives and hate liberals. If the people you love are all political progressives, it is the other way around. If you have a clear political leaning and you see a news story criticizing a member of your party or a policy you support, it can trigger strong emotions because it feels like your people are under attack.

---

11 | 2 Kings 21:1-9

Who your people are predisposes you to believe what your people believe. Consider the influence of who your people are on what you believe and what you value in the following list:

1. Gangs — If you belonged to a gang, would that affect the lens through which you looked at the world?

2. Cults — Most people in cults have no idea they are being deceived. Being with other people who look at life the same way makes the beliefs feel true.

3. Addicts — It is common for addicts to get clean while they are in a new environment, but to go back to their old lifestyle when they return to "their people."

4. Christians — Evangelicals, Charismatics, Catholics, and other groups within the Christian community often feel a sense of belonging with their group and distrust for others.

5. Atheists — If you grow up with people who see belief in God as a crutch at best and a delusion at worst, it is hard to break with your people to go in another direction.

6. Ethnic groups — Most ethnic groups have a sense of "us vs. them" built into their values. Some studies suggest that distrust of those who are "not my people" is hardwired into the brain and has to be overcome through maturity.

As you can see, there is almost no end to a list like this. Nearly all people groups see themselves as the center around which everyone else revolves. It should also be pointed out that belonging to a group not only gives you an identity by being in it, it affects how you see the other people groups. Being in a cult affects how you see Evangelicals. Being a New Ager affects how you see atheists. Rarely does someone inside a group see themselves in the same way that outsiders see them.

Who your people are creates your sense of identity. As soon as you say, "I belong to this group," you are giving yourself an identity. To say "I am an Evangelical" is a statement of both belonging and identity. If I am raised in that culture, I will be raised with a very clear narrative about life that will be radically different than if I am raised in a New Age culture or an agnostic household.

The following diagram helps us understand how attachments and beliefs form the values of a culture. Who my people are influences my worldview. The worldview I believe creates my values.

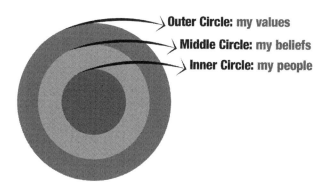

Outer Circle: my values
Middle Circle: my beliefs
Inner Circle: my people

The institutions of a culture (families, media, education, government, etc.) create belonging and teach worldview. Whoever controls the institutions of a culture can shape that culture through these foundational factors.

Attachments exert a powerful influence in shaping our beliefs and values. This is one of the reasons why we need to form healthy relationships with people who share the beliefs and values of the Bible. This is also why the Christian's identity is not simply rooted in beliefs, but in our attachment with God. The firmer that attachment, the more secure our identity will be.

Identity rooted in anything other than intimacy with God is like building a house on sinking sand. Attachment is the foundation of the house. Beliefs are like the walls that give it structure. When we have a sure foundation, our beliefs, emotions, and behaviors will be anchored to a secure foundation. When we have a faulty foundation, faulty beliefs, emotions, and behaviors flow.

Now that we have explored three core principles related to the influence of our beliefs on emotions and behavior, we want to introduce you to several tools you can use to begin winning the battle for your mind and taking control of your thought life.

TOOLS

Replacing Thoughts

We discussed this idea in the chapter on quieting. Now we want to introduce you to some specific strategies that can help you employ this tool. My friend Dr. Karl Payne is a discipleship expert and regular guest on the Janet Parshall radio broadcast. He also served as the chaplain of the Seattle Seahawks for over twenty years. According to Dr. Payne, when your thoughts are creating upsetting or unwanted emotions, a good strategy for dealing with the thought train that is driving us in a negative direction is to replace those thoughts.[12]

Too often, when we are feeling upset or overwhelmed, we just try to stop thinking about what is distressing us. It can be like playing mental "whack-a-mole." It is often hard to simply stop thinking about something upsetting. It can be like saying, "Don't think about the mean thing your boss said. Don't think about it. Stop thinking about what a

---

12 | Karl I. Payne, *Spiritual Warfare: Christians, Demonization, and Deliverance* (Washington DC: WND Books, 2011) pp. 78-80.

horrible thing he said." That strategy simply reinforces the negative thinking.

Instead of simply trying to stop negative thoughts, we need to focus on replacing them with something else. Dr. Payne uses a simple analogy. If you can't stop thinking about pink elephants wearing green booties, try thinking about white polar bears waltzing on an iceberg in the middle of the Atlantic. However, he also points out that if you can't successfully replace your thoughts, you may be dealing with a warfare situation that requires more direct confrontation with the enemy.

Sometimes, when you have trouble falling asleep because of the thoughts that race through your head, it can be a good strategy to focus on something completely different. This accomplishes two benefits: 1) It distracts you from what is upsetting, and 2) it gives you something positive to think about. For example, Judy Dunagan—a women's ministry specialist who often teaches on spiritual warfare and the battle for the mind—suggests going through the alphabet as you are trying to fall asleep and thinking of a title for God or Jesus related to each letter of the alphabet.[13]

Almighty
Benevolent
Christ
Door (I am the door to the sheep pen.)
El Shaddai
(Etc.)

Dr. Daniel Amen is a well-known brain science expert who has often appeared on television specials to talk about emotional health and the brain. He often advocates the idea of turning your brain into an "anteater." In fact, if you

---

13 | See Judy Dunagan's presentation "Spiritual Warfare Praying" on the Deeper Walk Streaming Service—recorded at Denver Seminary 2019.

visit his office, you will find all sorts of anteater decorations (I've heard he even has a live anteater in his main office).[14] Clearly, Dr. Amen wants people to ask, "What's up with all the anteaters?" He likes this question because it allows him to explain the idea of ANTs—automatic negative thoughts.

ANTs works like this. Whenever you feel one of the SAD-SAD emotions (or something similar) your brain automatically goes down a well-rehearsed path of supporting beliefs that fuel your negative emotion. So, perhaps when you feel angry with your boss, your mind automatically starts rehearsing thoughts like, "He always does this! Why does he have to be this way? I hate him!"

Turning your brain into an anteater starts by identifying these ANTs (Automatic Negative Thoughts). You can use a T-Bar chart like the one below.

Emotion: anger with my boss[15]

ANTs	ANT-eater
HE ALWAYS DOES THIS.	I DON'T HAVE TO MATCH HIS IMATURITY.
WHY DOES HE HAVE TO BE THIS WAY?	HE GETS LIKE THIS WHEN HIS RELATIONAL CIRCUITS ARE OFF. I DON'T KNOW HIS WHOLE STORY.
I HATE HIM.	...WHEN I'M NOT BEING MYSELF. BUT IN THE SPIRIT I CAN LOVE HIM.

---

14 | The anteater theme is so fundamental to Dr. Amen's approach he even has a children's book on the subject, *Captain Snout and the Super Power Questions: Don't Let the ANTs Steal Your Happiness* (Zonderkidz, 2017). See also, "The Number One Habit To Develop In Order To Feel More Positive" at Amenclinics. com (posted August 16, 2016).

15 | The statements in the T-Bar chart are for illustration only. There can often be more than one counter-statement to the automatic negative thought, and the answers are specific to each person and situation.

The idea behind this process is to come up with a game plan for common emotions that cause you trouble. If you often feel anxiety, then draw up a T-Bar chart about the most common negative thoughts you have when you feel that emotion. Once you have listed them, write another list of anteater thoughts you can focus on instead. This will help you create a battle strategy for taking thoughts captive and make it easier to replace your negative thoughts with positive ones.

One of the first times I (Marcus) assigned a T-Bar chart to someone was as a pastor working with a woman whose son had died tragically in a car accident. I encouraged her to start everyday by writing in a notebook the answer to the question, "What lie is the devil telling me today that needs to be renounced?" Then answering the question, "What is the truth God wants me to hold onto today?" Several years later she sent me a kind note thanking me for the assignment and said, "It probably saved my life."

Resisting the Devil

Not every thought that enters your head is yours. Some thoughts come from the Holy Spirit. Other thoughts can come from the devil, who is the father of lies. If you are battling thoughts from the enemy, you will find it difficult if not impossible to simply replace them. You will need to actively resist the devil and make him flee. You might make a declaration like this: "In the name of Jesus, I command whatever spirit has been assigned to make me angry (or some other emotion) to leave now. I reject your lies and your assignment to torment me."

Once you have resisted the enemy, ask God to help you replace the thoughts with something from Him. In some cases, thoughts may be deeply embedded in painful memories. When this is the case, it may take more than a declaration to make the enemy leave. It will likely require experiencing God's healing of the pain from the past through REAL prayer or something similar.

Rhyming Thoughts

Dr. Jim Wilder has made an interesting observation based on Hebrew poetry.[16] In Hebrew, poets don't worry about making words rhyme, but they do want their *thoughts* to rhyme. We see this in the book of Psalms: the second line of a verse often restates the idea of the first line or takes that idea and builds on it.

Just as thoughts rhyme in Hebrew poetry, God wants our thoughts to rhyme with His. When our thinking is in sync with His thinking, it brings us peace. When our thinking is out of line with God's thinking, it creates chaos. It is easy to become double-minded. James warns us that a double-minded man is unstable in all his ways. One form of double-minded living happens when part of our thinking is in sync with God and part of our thinking isn't.

The goal of thought rhyming combines our beliefs and our relational connection with God. We talk to Him about our emotions or our circumstances, and we pay attention to the thoughts we get in response. This helps us sort out the thoughts that need to be replaced from the thoughts that bring us peace. The more we focus on the thoughts that bring us peace, the more in sync with God we get.

One way to practice thought rhyming is to ask God to show you in words or pictures how you are being tempted to see a person who bothers you. Notice what image or thoughts come to mind and how they make you feel. Chances are they do not spur you toward love and joy. Then

---

16 | E. James Wilder, Anna Kang, John Loppnow, Sungshim Loppnow, *Joyful Journey: Listening to Immanuel* (Shepherd's House, Inc., 2015) pp. 33-38.

ask God for words or pictures about how He wants you to see this person. If your thoughts are in sync with God's thoughts, it should produce peace and create a greater desire to be loving.

THE POWER OF BELIEFS

In his book, *Could It Be This Simple?* psychiatrist Timothy Jennings describes the power of beliefs by documenting study after study showing how what we believe can have profound effects on how our body reacts.[17]

1. In one test, 100% of women with stomach nausea during pregnancy experienced complete remission of the symptoms when they believed they were taking a medicine to cure it. They were actually taking ipecac—a syrup intended to cause vomiting. Simply believing the medicine would work affected all of them.

2. In another placebo experiment, one group of people recovering from the swelling of wisdom tooth extraction were given a placebo. The other group received no treatment. 35% of those in the placebo group experienced less swelling, simply by believing the medicine would work.

3. A Japanese experiment blindfolded a group of boys then scratched both of their arms with tree branches. One of the branches created red, itchy bumps, the other didn't. In each case the boy developed the classic symptoms on the arm he thought had been brushed by the irritating branch, not the arm that had actually been brushed by the irritant.

---

17 | Timothy R. Jennings, *Could It Be This Simple? A Biblical Model for Healing the Mind* (Chattanooga: Lennox, 2012) pp. 12-13.

These studies and more have shown again and again that "the mind exerts an overwhelming power over the body."[18] In the same way that our beliefs can have a profound impact on our bodies, they can have a profound impact on our emotions and our behavior. It is no wonder that the Bible has so much to say about meditating on God's Word, renewing the mind, repenting, thinking about what is true, practicing gratitude, studying, and guarding what our minds think and believe.

A JOY WORKOUT

This joy workout will focus on storytelling.

1.   Write a bullet-pointed outline of your life asking one question, "How has God provided for me in times of need at various stages of my life?" For example,

> » God provided for me (Marcus) to be raised in a unique family as the son of Timothy and Eleanor Warner. That introduced me to many influential people and a great deal of cutting-edge Evangelical thought. It also gave me a stable home life.

> » God provided good friends and many happy memories at a private Christian school.

> » God provided free tuition for both college and seminary.

> » God gave me a job teaching college that I hadn't even know was open to apply for. That job gave me a platform and credibility that exist to this day.

> » God provided a wife who loves Him and loves partnering in ministry.

> » God provided miraculously for our rent early in our marriage through three unexpected gifts that all arrived the same day.

The list goes on and on.

---

18 | *Could It Be This Simple?*, p. 13.

2.   Once you've made a list like this, write out the answer to this question: "What does my experience teach me about what God is up to in my life?" In my case, I wrote:

> "God has clearly called me and prepared me for ministry. He put me in a special family, gave me education and credentials, connected me to the right people all along the way. His provision tells a story of calling."

3.   Close by writing a prayer of thanks for God's provision throughout your life.

CHAPTER SEVEN
connecting with people

As infants we rely on other people to create belonging for us. We don't know what we need or how to ask for it. Therefore, we depend on other people to recognize our needs and take care of us. In our childhood years, we begin to learn how to take care of ourselves, practice relational skills, and create friendships. By the time we are young adults, we should have developed the skills to form belonging with other people no matter where we go. If you go to a new school, you know how to engage with others and form connections. If you move to a new city, you have the skills to form new relationships and even create a sense of belonging for others. However, a lot of us never developed those skills. Whether because of A Trauma (the absence of the good we need) or B Trauma (the bad stuff that happens to us) or both, we often find ourselves in an adult world without the skills to form belonging. As a result, we are stuck hoping someone else will create it for us.

In this chapter we will explain two key principles for creating belonging with others and introduce several practical relational skills for connecting with people.

THE IMPORTANCE OF BELONGING

Belonging is key to building bounce. I need to feel like I have a people who will go through anything with me. Knowing that I belong to a group gives me the security of knowing that I don't have to go through hardship alone.

This is true of teams, military units, families, churches, and any other group you can name.

One of the most iconic teen movies of the 1980s was "The Breakfast Club." It was about five kids from different worlds who had to serve detention together on a Saturday. Four of the teens had a clear sense of belonging to a group. One was a jock, one a preppy girl, one a nerd, one a "metal head," and one was a loner who had no group. Knowing which group they were in gave them a clear sense of identity. Their identity created a clear set of values. Part of those values included a set of unwritten rules about how you treat "insiders" vs. "outsiders." For example, the preppy, pretty, homecoming queen knew who her people were. She was the ultimate insider and hung out with other kids from wealthy families who were good looking, high achievers. Belonging let her know who she spent time with and who she avoided. The jock also knew who his people were and who didn't belong in his group. Without being taught, he instinctively knew what the rules were for treating "outsiders" and "insiders." He admitted to bullying kids who were weak just because it was expected. Each of the students knew who their people were, which gave them an identity and code for how they lived their lives.

CONNECTING WITH PEOPLE IS CRUCIAL TO EMOTIONAL HEALTH.

The plot twist in this movie happened as these kids from different groups formed a sense of belonging with one another and formed their own group. Suddenly, the old rules went out the window about who you treated well and who you would even consider befriending. By the end of the movie their new sense of belonging had given them a new sense of identity and, with it, a new perspective on life.

Connecting with people is crucial to emotional health. Most of the clients who don't recover in spite of extensive therapy and spiritual intervention (like spiritual warfare and inner healing) are those who don't learn how to build belonging. One such person, who has come a long way in building the skills to connect well with others, calls himself "a recovering vampire." He doesn't mean he was in a secret occult group. He means his lack of skills in making connections and building belonging made him the sort of person who moved from relationship to relationship "sucking" the life out of people—like a relational/emotional vampire. Much of his healing journey has been about learning "connecting skills." The more these skills have grown, the easier it has been for him to feel safe, calm, and connected.

PRINCIPLE 1: VULNERABILITY

There are two keys to building belonging with others. The first is vulnerability. The second is empathy. Vulnerability is about letting others see the real you—weakness and all. Brené Brown, one of the most widely read authors on vulnerability, says simply: "Courage starts with showing up and letting ourselves be seen."[1] Without vulnerability there is no authenticity in a relationship, and without authenticity there can be no intimacy.

There is an obvious conflict that comes with being vulnerable and letting others see the real you including your weakness. It isn't always safe to be vulnerable. There is shame involved and a sense of danger that comes with it. Most social anxiety is related to a fear that vulnerability will be met with rejection. It is the fear that if people see the real you they won't want you to belong. When people fear the

---

1 | Brené Brown. *Daring Greatly: How the Courage to Be Vulnerable Transforms the Way We Live, Love, Parent, and Lead.* (New York: Gotham Books, 2012).

response to vulnerability, they settle for "fitting in" rather than creating true belonging.[2] Again, Brené Brown writes,

> Vulnerability is the birthplace of love, belonging, joy, courage, empathy, and creativity. It is the source of hope, empathy, accountability, and authenticity. If we want greater clarity in our purpose or deeper and more meaningful spiritual lives, vulnerability is the path.[3]

One of the skill-sets that everyone needs to develop is the art of authenticity. We need to learn how to share our heart at appropriate levels in appropriate situations. Just as there is an art to talking to children in age appropriate ways, there is an art to being vulnerable at appropriate levels.

The key factor to determining what is appropriate is the maturity level of the other person. There is some weakness I won't share with an emotional infant or even an emotional child. I will only share it with an adult. There is some weakness I don't want to share with anyone other than an elder. I do this partly to protect the other person. I don't want to lay a burden on them heavier than they can handle. I also do this in part to protect myself, because infants and children are far more likely to attack my weakness when they are overwhelmed. I am not saying I act fake or wear a mask around children, but I do limit the amount of weakness I share.

A second key factor to determining what is appropriate is context. If you are paying for a counseling appointment you are free to share a whole lot more than if you are standing in line at a fast food restaurant.

Vulnerability is about the desire to be seen. Some of us have learned not to trust vulnerability because we have

---

2 | *Daring Greatly*
3 | *Daring Greatly*, p. 34.

been wounded in our desire to be seen. This is inevitable at some level because we live in a broken world full of broken people.

The problem with vulnerability

Each person's story contains a profound conflict. Two truths stand side by side, waging war against the other. The first truth is that we enter this world completely vulnerable and dependent on others to meet even our most basic needs. The second truth, which we cannot escape, is that we live in a broken and fallen world. We are at the mercy of broken people. Therefore, each of us at some point will be missed, disappointed, misunderstood, mistreated and/or neglected. In between these two truths is a space. Shame loves to rush in and fill the space between with colorful narratives.

Shame is a disconnector. When we feel shame, it sends a cascade of disconnecting beliefs and emotions that can saturate a person's whole being. It makes you feel detached from your heart, thoughts, feelings, and identity. Shame also sends signals to your true self to hide, which makes you feel even more disconnected from God and others.

Every time our God-given needs for connection, love, and safety are not met, we become susceptible to believing the narratives that shame spins. Consider these examples.

» A little girl stands before her daddy in a new dress with hopeful anticipation. She wants to hear, "You look beautiful!" but instead, she gets distracted dismissal. At that moment, shame rushes in to say, "See, you are not lovely. No one will ever think you are beautiful."

» A little boy afraid of a thunderstorm runs to his parents looking for reassurance. Instead he hears, "Don't be a baby, go back to bed." In that instant, shame whispers in his ear, "You are a baby. You will never measure up. You will always fall short."

Whether your family of origin was loving, abusive, or somewhere in between, there are places where shame rushed in to tell you an ugly story.

According to Curt Thompson in his book *The Soul of Shame*, we have a God-given need to be seen, known, and loved for who we are without fear of rejection. However, we each intrinsically understand that the more of me that is exposed to another, the more at risk I am to experiencing pain.[4] This is a conflict that we attempt to solve in a number of ways. We may hide, run, fight, or try to please.

If exposing our weaknesses feels dangerous, we may set out to exterminate vulnerability. We may try to control how others see us, hide away the messy parts. But what if vulnerability isn't a sign that something is wrong with me? What if it is how I was created? What if God intentionally created us as vulnerable beings because we were never meant to do life on our own? What if we can't do life without God and without others? What if embracing my vulnerability is actually the bridge that brings the connection my heart has been longing for? We cannot feel loved if we do not feel known, and we cannot feel known if we are not seen.

Many researchers have concluded that the degree to which I am able to invite people into the messy places in my life is directly proportional to whether or not I feel connected and loved.[5] I may feel safer hidden behind my protective walls, but I will not feel loved and connected to others. If I am not connected authentically, I will not feel connected deeply, and a life filled with shallow connections will make it nearly impossible to live with joy.

---

4 | Curt Thompson, *The Soul of Shame* (Downers Grove: InterVarsity Press, 2015).

5 | Research includes articles like "Shame, status, and social roles: Psychobiology and evolution." by P. Gilbert & B. Andrews (Eds). *Series in affective science. Shame: Interpersonal behavior, psychopathology, and culture* (pp. 99–125). Oxford University Press (1998). In this article, the authors argue that shame triggers involuntary submissive behavior in which subordinates (or those who see themselves as subordinates) automatically defer to those who are dominant.

Shame in the Bible

Shame is one of the first emotions we see in the Bible. When God came looking for Adam and Eve after they sinned, He asked "Where are you?" He wasn't asking because He was ignorant of their physical location. He was looking to reestablish connection with them. In their shame, Adam and Eve ran, hid, and covered themselves. They then blamed the other for the fall. They disconnected from God and each other. How often in our own shame do we do the same thing?

Jesus, however, had a different plan. He killed an animal, shedding its blood, and covered Adam and Eve in the sacrifice. In the very places where we try to disconnect from others in our shame, Jesus wants to be invited in. Jesus wants to enter into the places in our story we have covered up and tried to hide. Jesus is the embodiment of God's plan to reestablish connection with us. He is the bridge. He came into this world as a naked baby, the most vulnerable form there is. He gave Himself into the hands of those who hated Him. He became vulnerable so He could become the bridge that allows us to reconnect with God.

JESUS IS THE EMBODIMENT OF GOD'S PLAN TO REESTABLISH CONNECTION WITH US.

This is the essence of reconciliation. It is the fruit of an extravagant love that enters the most vulnerable places in our hearts and brings the gifts of kindness and mercy. Once we have been the recipient of a grace that meets our vulnerability with kindness, we want to show the same kind of grace to others. This is what empathy does. It extends grace to others in order to create authentic connection. Since Jesus, Son of the Most High God, has met us with grace in the places of our deepest shame, how can we help but extend the same grace to others?

Jesus was not afraid to be in relationship with the prostitute, leper, and morally corrupt. I am convinced when He looks at us, He sees our truest self—who He created us to be.

He also sees our broken heart. He knows His children and the mountain of wounding they've been buried under. The good news is that He is still in the business of loving the unlovable. He isn't afraid to step into our story and love us where we are, stepping into the darkest places of the human heart and bringing hope, healing, and restoration.

In my (Stefanie's) counseling practice, I work with survivors of complex childhood abuse. Over the years, I have had opportunities to meet several men and woman whose lives seemed to be defined by the shame they carry. I've walked with many who are marginalized from society because the effects of trauma seem to mark them with a scarlet A.

A few years ago, I had an opportunity to get to know a young woman who, because of her trauma, was unable to hold a job. She had been kicked out of several churches and ministries for being a "Jezebel." Shame followed her everywhere she went. Yet she loved Jesus. She felt like a leper. She vowed never to step foot in another church but faithfully watched sermons online and worshiped Him on her own. Loneliness plagued her life, but being alone had proven safer than engaging people. She lacked skills to do healthy relationship. I watched as week after week Jesus entered into painful scenes from her life and brought truth, love, and healing.

After a long battle and years of faithfully journeying with Jesus on the healing path, this young woman found freedom. She is now a leader in a healing ministry. Jesus sees us. He knows who we are, even when the world labels us outcast. He goes after the least of these. I believe, as the hands and feet of Jesus, the Church should also be equipped to love the unlovable well. They, too, have important Kingdom work to do.

PRINCIPLE 2: EMPATHY

Transparency and authenticity create trust. Trust is essential, but there is something else that plays an important role in forming deep, meaningful connections, and that is empathy. We really cannot talk about empathy without understanding shame. Shame is what makes people run, hide, and blame, but empathy is what draws them back out. Dr. Brené Brown says, "If you put shame in a petri dish, it needs three ingredients to grow exponentially: secrecy, silence, and judgment. If you put the same amount of shame in the petri dish and douse it with empathy, it can't survive."[6]

Empathy is really nothing more than connecting with someone in their shame and clothing them with dignity, just like God did for Adam and Eve. So how do we become empathetic? How do we learn to connect with others in their pain? I (Stefanie) will be the first to say that walking with others through pain is very messy. I have made many mistakes, but I've learned a few things, too. I would like to share some helpful tools to responding well.

> **EMPATHY IS REALLY NOTHING MORE THAN CONNECTING WITH SOMEONE IN THEIR SHAME AND CLOTHING THEM WITH DIGNITY.**

The moment after someone is brave and shares from a place of vulnerability, shame will be present. This is also the place where empathy can make a big difference. I (Marcus) got to hear Stefanie model empathy with a lady I had been trying to help by phone for quite some time. I invited Stefanie to join our call one day, and this woman shared the story of a family that had made her their emotional "whipping post" for years. Stefanie listened to the story and the pain being expressed and blurted out, "Wow,

---

6 | From the TED Talk "Listening to Shame" www.happify.com/hd/powerful-antidote-to-shame-brene-brown/

that just makes my mother's heart angry! The momma bear in me wants to say, 'That's not right, you can't treat her like that.'" It was a powerful moment for the woman on the other end of the line. She had been waiting her whole life for a mother to say those words.

In reflecting on that phone call, I noticed the difference between validation and empathy. Stefanie didn't simply validate and affirm that she was hearing a lot of pain, she took the next step and showed empathy by expressing the strong emotions being created in her. Authentic emotion was met with authentic emotion.

A person sharing for the first time is like a turtle peeking out of its shell. If the responses are empathic and kind, the person will come out of their shell further and risk sharing more. However, if the responses are cookie cutter or invalidating the sharer may shut down, retreat back into their shell, and vow never to share again.

I (Stefanie) have heard it said (and I tend to agree) that the difference between suffering and trauma is whether we feel alone in it or not. I believe it is important that we learn to enter into people's pain in an empathetic way so they hear from us: "I might not understand exactly what it was like for you, but I see you and I care enough to sit with you as you tell your story." It is important to let them name what happened to them, let your heart connect with their story, and offer kindness. It is important to learn how to respond well to others in these moments.

4 Relational Skill Sets

Learning how to build belonging requires learning some essential relational skills. Some of you already have these skills, but you may not have the language to explain them to others who may need to learn them. The acronym CAKE can provide that language.

Skill Set #1: CAKE: turning on your relational circuits

In our book *The 4 Habits of Joy-Filled Marriages*, Chris Coursey and I (Marcus) talk about an on/off switch in the brain. When your switch is on, your relational circuits engage and your right brain skills are free to operate. However, when your switch shuts off (often because you get triggered, but sometimes just from being preoccupied or tired), your relational circuits shut down and you lose access to several crucial parts of brain function. These functions include acting like yourself, regulating your emotions, returning to joy, and remaining relational.

To help you recognize when your relational circuits are off, and to give you strategies for getting them back on, we use the word CAKE.[7]

Curiosity. When our relational circuits are on, we are naturally curious about how other people feel, what they have been up to, and what they are thinking. If we find that we are not curious, it is a good sign that our switch has turned off and our relational circuits have shut down. It's also worth noting that the left-brain version of curiosity is sarcasm. Saying or thinking, "I'm curious, are you always this stupid?" is not going to help the situation or get your relational circuits reengaged.

Appreciation. When we are using our whole brain—and not just half of it because our switch has shut off our relational circuits—it is easy to find qualities and actions to appreciate about other people. However, when our switch goes off, it is easy to forget what we like about someone. As a result, we may find ourselves treating a friend more like an enemy. Choosing to find something to appreciate is a good strategy

---

7 | The CAKE acrostic used here is taken from Marcus Warner and Chris Coursey's book *The 4 Habits of Joy-Filled Marriages* (Chicago: Northfield 2019) p. 36. There is another version of CAKE in *Rare Leadership* by Marcus Warner and Jim Wilder (Chicago: Moody 2016) pp. 129-134. In *Rare Leadership* E stands for Envelope Conversations. These are discussed as a separate skill set in this chapter.

for flipping the switch in our brain and getting our circuits back on.

Kindness. One of the bestselling Christian books of all time is *The Five Love Languages* by Gary Chapman. The love languages he describes can be thought of as ways to be kind to someone. Kindness is a choice we can make to help get our relational circuits back online. Chapman presents each of the five love languages as choices we can make. The love languages are words of affirmation, gifts, acts of service, quality time, and physical touch.

Eye Contact. When our relational circuits are off, it is easy to stop looking people in the eye in order to avoid feeling connected. The opposite is also true. Choosing to make eye contact can help us get our relational circuits re-engaged.

When you recognize that you're "offline" and can't practice the CAKE skills naturally, there is a simple strategy you can follow to get back "online."

1. **Take a break.** Disengage. Intentionally look away from the person and use your left-brain, problem-solving skills to figure out how to get your right brain re-engaged. Sometimes you can do this quickly—in under a minute. Sometimes you need a longer break and may even need to end a conversation so you can postpone the discussion until a later time, when your switch is on.

2. **Use your left brain to solve the problem of how to get your relational circuits back on.** While you are disengaged relationally, focus your problem-solving left brain on the task of finding some curiosity, appreciation, or kindness. This requires recognizing that half of your brain has shut down and addressing the problem of how to get it back on.

3. Re-engage with eye contact and use one of the first three strategies—curiosity, appreciation, or kindness.

Skill Set #2: VCR: Validate, Comfort, Recover[8]

We introduced VCR in chapter one, but I want to take a closer look at this important skill set. Several years ago, my wife and I had the opportunity to spend the day driving through the Colorado Rockies with Jim and Kitty Wilder. I (Marcus) couldn't resist the opportunity to pick Jim's brain on a few topics. One of the subjects that came up was how to train people with the relational skills necessary to recover from upsetting emotions. While we were enjoying the majestic scenery, he taught me a simple process that has had a profound impact on many lives. It is the VCR process described in chapter one. The letters VCR stand for Validate, Comfort, and Recover.

Jim told me about a counseling center that always had two workers present, either in person or on the phone, whenever anyone came to them for help. The first person had only one job—validate every emotion expressed. The second person had only one job—after the validation help make the problem smaller.

Validation simply meant accurately naming the emotion being expressed and accurately identifying how big that emotion was for the person. It wasn't their job to fix or agree with anything, just to be accurate. Giving a name to what the person was feeling helped them feel seen and understood. They felt validated.

Comforting was not about fixing a problem but about making it smaller. The way you do this will look different with a child than with an adult. With a child, you may have to help them find their words. With an adult, you may do

---

8 | In *Rare Leadership* R stands for "repattern." The word "repattern" emphasizes the need to learn the skill of recovery later in life.

this more interactively by asking questions and letting them draw their own conclusions, but the goal is the same, and that is to use these strategies to bring comfort by making the problem more manageable.

1. Tell the person what won't happen. Anxiety is rooted in imagination and often catastrophic imagination. It can be very helpful to have someone tell you what won't happen. Suppose you are trying to comfort a child who fell and hurt their knee. You might make the problem smaller by telling them what won't happen.

> » I see the blood, but it doesn't look too bad.
>
> » Don't worry, you aren't going to die. (If kids have never seen their own blood before this can be a real fear.)
>
> » We aren't going to have to take you to the doctor. We can handle this right here.
>
> » This doesn't look too deep. You aren't going to need stitches. (I, Marcus, had 27 stitches growing up, so I heard this a lot.)

2. Offer a new perspective. You can offer your own opinion about how the situation looks. In some cases, you may want to ask them how someone else (particularly someone they respect) might look at their situation. The goal is to find a way to get them to look at their situation from a perspective they haven't considered. This can be very simple, like, "I think you are going to be okay." It might take the form of a question, such as, "Is there any chance this could have been an accident, or are you sure they did this on purpose?" It can also be corrective, "Maybe the boy pushed you because you were being mean." There are many forms a new perspective can take.

3. **Help them develop a plan.** There is a time to make suggestions about how to fix a problem or how to make that problem smaller. As long as a person feels like their emotions have been validated, they are usually open to hearing opinions about next steps or possible fixes. You may need to validate more emotions along the way. Your suggestions might trigger anger, which will need to be validated. They may trigger fear, which will need to be validated. The process isn't always a straight line.

HAVING A PLAN GENERATES HOPE.

If the validating and comforting has worked, the person will begin to feel better. They may not be pain free, but they'll feel like they can handle what is in front of them.

According to Dr. Wilder, as people would go through this process again and again, they began to learn how to do it for themselves. Within a few months, even people with borderline diagnoses were beginning to master the skill of validating and comforting themselves so they could recover from a variety of upsetting emotions.

A few years ago, I (Marcus) was asked to be on a live radio program with a national audience. People were going to be calling in with problems that needed to be solved. To prepare myself for the program I had a pad of paper next to me with the letters "VCR" written across the top. It was a reminder to validate their emotions before trying to solve their problems.

During the interview, the topic of spiritual warfare had come up, and I had mentioned that spirit guides were demonic. Someone soon called in to challenge this point and argue that many spirit guides were good and helpful. Without the VCR reminder, I would have simply jumped in and started making my case. However, I started by saying, "It sounds like spirituality is very important to you and that you want to be open minded about practices that might be helpful to people. That is very admirable." My goal was to make her feel understood. The conversation became more relaxed after that. I was then able to tell her that according to the Bible there is only one Spirit Guide and that is the Holy Spirit. Other spirits may masquerade as angels of light, but you can tell the difference because of the fruit they produce. The conversation ended with her thanking me for the clarification.

When it comes to the VCR process, order and accuracy are very important. Validation has to come before comforting, and you need to be accurate in the way you name emotions. It is worth noting here that someone may be feeling several emotions at once and not just one.

For example, a child might be angry and scared and ashamed all at the same time. If my child wakes me up at night because she wet the bed, I have to be careful not to project my emotions onto her. Wetting the bed might make me feel shame, but I shouldn't simply assume that's the emotion she's feeling. She might be feeling something else. Perhaps she is afraid that she will get in trouble. Perhaps she is angry because someone made her drink a big glass of water before she went to bed. In order to validate an emotion, you need to make sure you validate the correct emotion.

Skill Set #3: Building relational trust on a continuum

As mentioned earlier, not every friendship needs to be an intimate friendship. Even Jesus had His most trusted relationships (inner circle), then a larger circle (the 12), then the greater church. It is good to have one or two people with whom we are free to share our heart with without fear of rejection, betrayal, or exposure.

I (Stefanie) feel absolutely free to share my heart uncensored with my husband. He is my most intimate relationship. I also have one or two friends in my life with whom I can share my heart without fear that they would change their mind about loving me, that they would make fun of me behind my back, or use what I shared against me. I am sure that their love for me is unconditional and that they are for me 100%, because I have many years of trust building with each of these people.

Trust builds like a dimmer switch slowly over time, but can be lost like a toggle switch. When we are first getting to know a new friend, it can be helpful to assess at what level we can trust them on a continuum rather than a yes or no. Many people try to determine this too quickly and can either become too intimate too soon or misjudge and end up hurt. Can I trust them with my hobbies? Can we hang out and play basketball or tennis? After I'm with them, do I feel encouraged and energized or drained and anxious?

If after spending some time with them, I feel like they were safe, I can try trusting them with a few stories from my childhood or something more personal. There are many levels of trust. The more you risk being seen, the more known you will feel. The more known you feel in the context of safe friendship, the more loved you will feel.

Skill Set #4: Envelope Conversations: processing conflict relationally

An envelope conversation is a tool for talking about problems. In too many cases, when we get frustrated or angry, we lead with the problem when we talk to people. You can think of this as leading with your left brain instead of taking the time to make a right-brain connection and having the goal of keeping your relationship bigger than the problem.

It should be pointed out that keeping relationships bigger than problems doesn't mean you will always solve the problem at hand. It doesn't even mean that you will always save the relationship. Jesus was not able to save His relationship with most of the religious leaders of His day. In fact, at one point, most of those following Him abandoned the relationship

(John 6:66). This was also true of the apostle Paul who part-ed ways with people or let them walk away when problems could not be solved.[9]

The goal of keeping relationships bigger than problems is to keep your relational circuits on when you need to talk about a problem. An envelope conversation is a good way to do this. It looks like this.

1. **Start with the history of your relationship.** Don't use this step to criticize the other person. You don't want to start with a statement like, "You've been unfair to me for a long time," or, "You never listen to me." That is not what we mean by starting with your relational history. It means saying things like, "You and I have known each other a long time," or, "You just moved in," or, "We've worked together for about three years now."

2. **Address the problem.** The problem could be as small as, "I wish you wouldn't set your water glass on the table without a coaster," or it can be as big as betrayal. It is a good idea to practice with smaller problems before going straight for the biggest issue in your relationship.

3. **State your hope for a good relationship in the future.** "I hope we will be able to work well together in future projects that come along." "However we solve this problem, I hope we have a great relationship moving forward."

---

9 | In John 6 many people stopped following Jesus, and He didn't go running after them. Jesus remained relational when He confronted His disciples or the Pharisees, but His relationship with Judas ended as did His relationship with many of the Pharisees. Paul confronted Peter about a problem, but with the clear goal of solving the problem not only for the sake of their relationship but for the unity of the church (Galatians 2). Paul was not opposed to splitting a church over heresy or unorthodox practice. He went so far as to command that certain people be put out of the church until they repented (1 Corinthians 5). We also see this with Jesus in the letters He dictated to John in the book of Revelation.

Envelope conversations are designed to help you stay relational when confrontation is needed. The tool was first developed by Jim Wilder as a "sandwich conversation." He used the analogy of putting the meat of the problem between two slices of relational bread.[10]

A JOY WORKOUT

We live in a world filled with lonely people. Many feel isolated with no hope of relational connection. Rather than wait for people to create belonging for us, we want to encourage people to learn how to create belonging for ourselves, to build relational connection wherever we go. Here are two simple exercises I (Marcus) learned from Jim Wilder.

Create three up and three down community.

The goal is to have three people upstream from you who have strengths you lack, but also to have three people downstream from you who benefit from strengths you provide.

No matter where you are on your healing journey, you have strength to offer someone who is weaker than you in some way. It may be volunteering in a soup kitchen, smiling at someone when you see them, or showing genuine curiosity in someone others ignore. Offering strength to people who need what you have to offer is an important part of connecting with others.

Receiving what others have to offer also keeps us humble, teachable, and bearable to others. If we only focus on offering our strengths and refuse to receive strength from others, we tend toward selfishness and narcissism.

---

10 | Dr. Wilder and I changed the analogy from sandwiches to envelopes when we wrote *Rare Leadership* because I needed an E for the word CAKE.

Chart routine connections.

It can be helpful to make a list of who you see regularly. For example, do you ride a bus and see the driver several times a week? Make a table like the example below and create a list of all the people you see regularly. We suggest using names in your table when you know them. If you don't know someone's name, finding out is a great way to instigate relationship.

Find a way to add a little joy to each relationship. The more sharing joy becomes a habit, the easier it is to build relational connections.

Daily/Often	Weekly	Monthly	Other
bus driver	teacher	social worker	parents
barista	grocery clerk	book club	other siblings
neighbor	Bible study	sister	accountant
postal worker			

Building bounce is all about feeling safe, calm, and connected. Practicing appreciation and taking thoughts captive are important skills, but what our brains crave most is connection. Practicing the skills that build secure attachments is crucial to long-term emotional health. In our final chapter we are going to look at how to build a secure attachment with the most important connection of all—our connection with God.

CHAPTER EIGHT
connecting with God

Max Lucado is a well-loved storyteller. One of his stories is about the time he lived through a hurricane while living on a houseboat in Miami.[1] Yes, I said a houseboat. Max was not used to hurricanes. He had not grown up near the ocean and wasn't sure how to get ready for the approaching monster. This was before the days of internet, so he couldn't look up a video on how to prepare your houseboat for a hurricane.

He and his friends did what they thought was the wise thing. They bought a bunch of rope and started tying his houseboat to every fixed, immovable object he could find—trees, fire hydrants, fences, etc.

Fortunately, a veteran of many storms came by and saw what he and his friends were doing. The experienced sailor took pity on them and warned the group that what they were doing wasn't going to work. It was just going to pull the houseboat apart when the storm hit.

"What do I do?" asked Max.

"You have to anchor deep," he said. The old sea salt told him to go out a ways from shore and drop anchors to four separate secure spots. "Give yourself plenty of slack," he continued, "that way when the storm hits and the waves toss your boat up and down and back and forth, it won't get torn apart."

---

1 | Max Lucado, *Six Hours One Friday* (Portland: Multnomah, 1989) pp. 1-4.

To use our terms, the houseboat would "bounce."

This story has always hit me at two levels.

1. Too many of us are looking for security in all the wrong places. We tie our lives to false hope. The kindest thing God can do in those cases is to help us break free from what has us bound. That can be a really hard thing to go through, especially if we are convinced that we can't live without whatever it is He is taking away.

2. Too few of us have a secure anchor to God—one that can hold firm during the storms of life. We need to anchor deep.

Why connecting with God matters

You often hear people say that Christianity is not a religion but a relationship. Yet, I wonder if we know what that really means? Relationships are attachments. Christianity is about forming an attachment with Jesus Christ, then spending the rest of your life going deeper in your walk with Him. In John, the apostle wrote, "Now this is eternal life: that they know you, the only true God, and Jesus Christ, whom you have sent."[2] The Greek word translated "to know" is a relational word. It doesn't mean to know *about* someone but to know them relationally. It implies a certain amount of intimacy.

We get a similar picture in John 15 when Jesus described our relationship to Him as branches attached to a vine. Jesus is the vine, because He is the source of life. We are branches because if we lose our connection to the vine, we lose our connection to the source of life and we die. In this foundational text, Jesus makes it clear that the whole Christian faith can be reduced to one essential component—abiding in Christ.

---

2 | John 17:3

From this perspective, **the entire Christian experience is about connection.** Our connection to God and our connection to others. This is why the two greatest commandments are 1) love the Lord your God and 2) love your neighbor as yourself.[3] All of God's instruction about life can be reduced to these two elements. Everything else—faith, works, knowledge, service, disciplines, prayer, evangelism, church—all of it supports the growth of these two essential connections. Our Christianity goes awry when our focus shifts from loving God and others to all of the other stuff. That is when Christianity becomes a burden. It can get distorted to the point that it becomes lifeless at best and abusive at worst.

TRYING TO BE A GOOD CHRISTIAN WITHOUT A STRONG CONNECTION TO JESUS CHRIST MISSES THE WHOLE POINT OF CHRISTIANITY.

Trying to be a good Christian without a strong connection to Jesus Christ misses the whole point of Christianity. If I spend my whole life trying to do good things to keep God happy or trying to do just enough to make sure that I get into heaven when I die, I've missed the point.

Eternal life is not a reward given on judgment day to those who have been good or to those who have believed the right things. Jesus is life. He spoke life into the world at Creation.[4] He will speak life into the dead at resurrection day.[5] He is the way, the truth, and the life.[6] This is why He is the vine, and we are the branches.[7] The life is in Him, not in us. We only experience the life He came to give as we bond to Him. Thus, salvation is primarily about attachment. We are saved through

3 | Matthew 22:36-40
4 | John 1:1-3
5 | John 5:24-30; John 11:25-26
6 | John 14:6
7 | John 15:1-5

the connection with Christ that is formed as we put our faith in Him and begin to do life with Him. We mature in our faith as that connection strengthens. This is why Paul wrote, "So then, just as you received Christ Jesus as Lord, continue to live your lives in him, rooted and built up in him, strengthened in the faith as you were taught, and overflowing with thankfulness."[8]

Establishing a connection

A connection with God can be as simple as the one established between Jesus and the thief on the cross. They made a connection. He bonded to the source of all life and thus received eternal life. The thief who died on the cross that day did not have a chance to mature in his faith and grow his connection, but simply making the connection was enough to bring him into God's kingdom.

> REPENTANCE IS A HAPPY WORD BECAUSE IT MEANS THERE IS HOPE FOR THE FUTURE.

Jesus summed up the process of establishing a connection with Him in one word: repentance. Now, that word has often been grossly misunderstood and misused. For many of us the idea of repentance is connected to toxic shame, fear, and even abuse. We have had pastors and leaders threaten us and shame us in the hope that we will repent. However, even though I don't remember who he was, I (Marcus) agree with the preacher who said, "Repentance is the happiest word in the English language." Repentance is a happy word because it means there is hope for the future and that my sins and follies are not the end of the story.

Jesus said, "Repent, for the kingdom of heaven is at hand."[9] This is Matthew's favorite summary of the Gospel message. Repentance is the entry point into relationship with Jesus because it demonstrates the humility needed to admit we are on

8 | Colossians 2:6-7
9 | Matthew 4:17 (see also 3:2 and 10:7)

the wrong path and that we are separated from Christ and His kingdom. To repent doesn't mean we suddenly become perfect and stop making mistakes or even that we stop sinning. To repent means that we humbly admit the way we are doing life isn't working and we need to be connected to Jesus. It is the conviction that, in following Jesus, He will begin to strip away what is out of step with His heart and His kingdom, and He will begin to grow in me the love and perspective of His Father.

The invitation of Jesus is simply this, "Come follow me, and I will lead you on a new path." As we follow Him, we establish a connection. When we get baptized, we announce our connection to our fellow believers. As we continue to follow Him, we grow our connection, and a big connection creates a tremendous amount of emotional capacity for dealing with the hardships of life.

Growing our connection

A big connection with Jesus develops as we mature. If you have ever visited a vineyard, you know that the goal of the caretakers is to grow vines that have short branches. They prune the branches to keep them short. This helps to create a large connection with the vine that can be as big as a human fist.[10] A big connection lets lots of sap flow from the vine into the branch. A short branch forces that sap into the grapes, so they get big and juicy. If you have a small connection, then only a little sap gets into the branch. If you have a long branch, the sap is not as concentrated, so your grapes tend to be smaller and less juicy. If the branch gets broken off of the vine, nothing grows at all.

Caretakers rely on two key elements to grow this type of connection between a vine and its branches: pruning

---

10 | For a good summary of the grape growing process see Bruce Wilkinson *Secrets of the Vine: Breaking Through to Abundance* (Colorado Springs: Multnomah, 2001).

and time. Pruning keeps the branches short. This forces more sap into the grapes. It also grows the point of connection between the branch and the vine. Over time, vines with regularly pruned branches become mature and routinely grow lots of big, juicy grapes.

This is the analogy that Jesus used to help us understand the importance of our connection to Him and how that connection grows. There is an obvious relationship between abiding in Christ, pruning, and building bounce. Building bounce is about enduring hardship well, and God's pruning in our lives often involves going through hardship. Pruning isn't simply about suffering physically or emotionally. Pruning takes place at those times in our lives when God forces us to deal with issues that are keeping us from a deeper walk with Him. We all need pruning. It may be related to pride or addiction or shame or fear or anger or any number of other issues. No matter what it is, the pruning process is about making our lives smaller. God prunes in order to eliminate distractions and distortions that keep us from growing a strong connection to the vine.

HEARING FROM GOD

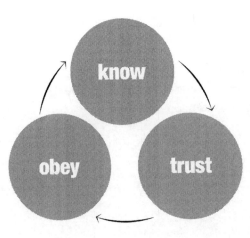

The keys to growing a deeper walk with God can be pictured as a triangle in which knowing God leads to trusting Him more. Trusting God leads to obeying Him more, and obeying God leads to knowing Him more.

It is hard to trust someone you don't know. However, choosing to trust God so that you obey Him and do what

He says lets us watch how He works and helps us know Him better.

Growing in our ability to trust God allows us to quiet ourselves and appreciate God's presence in the world around us. As we have already seen, quieting and appreciation are essential ingredients to building bounce. A second key to a deeper walk with God is developing the ability to hear God's voice.

If we wait until God blinds us with a flash of light and shows up in a vision the way He did with Paul on the Damascus road, we may find ourselves waiting for a while. That type of dramatic experience tends to be reserved for those who are called into a ministry that will require great sacrifice. Paul had such an experience and had to go through great hardship. Many prophets who endured great opposition had similar experiences. Isaiah saw the Lord surrounded by seraphim in the temple. Moses heard God in a burning bush. Samuel heard God speak to him as a child. As a teenager, Jeremiah had a vision of God.

The normal Christian life, even the day-to-day experience of people like Moses, Samuel, Jeremiah, and Paul, is one of learning to trust God with hard situations and to experience the connection of hearing the still small voice within.

When I (Stefanie) was growing up, I had no expectation that God would speak to me. Therefore, I never learned to listen. Later in life, however, I learned that I often missed God's voice because it sounds much like all the other thoughts in my head. With time I learned to pay attention to my thoughts and recognize the ones that come from Him.

My journey with hearing God has been long. I remember the first time I heard someone teach on God's sheep knowing His voice. I panicked and thought, "Maybe I'm not really a Christian." I asked God to teach me to hear His voice. That started a conversation that is still going on today. Sometimes

I'm sure that I'm hearing Him, and sometimes I doubt. What I know for sure is that He is always guiding me, and I don't have to hear Him perfectly to trust Him. I will share a few things that I have learned on my journey.

One day as I was driving and lamenting to God about something that was bothering me, I felt in my spirit that God was tapping me on the shoulder in some way. It stopped me in my tracks and made me smile.

I said, "What was that?"

He said (not audibly but like concepts dropping into my understanding), "Honey, I'm right here."

I said, "What do you mean?"

He clarified, "You are praying to Me like I'm out there somewhere, but I'm right here. It helps to know where I am when you are talking to Me." He was right.

Have you ever been talking to someone and they walk out of the room mid-story? You call out, "Where did you go?" and they say something like, "I can still hear you." It's so frustrating, because it feels like they aren't really listening. I prayed like that with God all my life. I would throw up prayers and hope He could hear me.

This day the Lord corrected this for me. He taught me that He is sitting as close to me as a person can sit, giving me direct eye contact, and listening intently to my every word. Turns out God is a very good listener. In fact, He has perfect listening skills. Now, I imagine Him nodding in all the right places, and, when I tell Him about my pain, He cries with me. This has changed how I pray.

In prayer, I love to ask for God's perspective. I know that my perspective is flawed, but His often changes the narrative on a dime. I love perspective shifts that radically change the current narrative from doom to redemption. Sometimes I get pictures that tell a story, but most of the time I just hear a voice in my head that could be easily mistaken for my own. I only know it's Him because He is way wiser than me, and the thoughts seems to come from outside of my own stream of thought. I can be thinking about things that run together with connecting thoughts and then out of nowhere an idea will drop that doesn't fit with my own train of thought. When it's from God, it will always reflect His character and never contradict His word.

Another prayer I like to pray is for strategy. I believe God has a strategy for everything. He is just waiting for us to ask. I can tell you many stories about coming to the end of my own mind on an issue and then asking God for strategy. Manna from heaven comes when we are stuck between two impossible choices. He loves to part the sea, walk on water, calm the storm. We just have to ask.

I (Marcus) have been in many counseling situations as a pastor when I came to the end of what I knew to do. On one occasion, I remember telling the person, "You have so many issues, it feels like we are dealing with a spaghetti bowl full of noodles where the noodles represent problems. I don't know which noodle to pull out first." So we stopped and prayed, "God, would you show us which of these issues you want to tackle first?"

I asked the lady to tell me the first problem that came to her mind. She did, then she started to mention a second one, and I stopped her. "Let's just address one at a time. Let's start with the issue you just raised." It turned out to be a classic wound, lie, vow, stronghold pattern,[11] and I was able to help her connect with Jesus to get healing for that pain.

Once we had connected with Jesus, we were able to ask Him, "Where do You want us to go next?" He brought up one memory at a time and walked us through His strategy

---

11 | This pattern is explained in *Understanding the Wounded Heart* by Marcus Warner.

for unraveling her mess. By the end of that two-hour session, Jesus had met her in about four different memories, and she was feeling much more peace than when we started. He knew just the right strategy for the time we had that day.

PRACTICING LISTENING PRAYER

In the book *Liberating Prayer*, Neil T. Anderson describes the day he learned to practice listening prayer. He was teaching a series on prayer based on a classic book, and the title of the last chapter was "How to Pray in the Spirit." This was troubling to him, because, in his own words, "I didn't have the foggiest idea how to pray by the Spirit."[12] As he struggled that night, Jesus met him and led him to two important discoveries.

1) Prayer needs to involve active listening. That night he prayed, "Okay, Lord—I'm setting aside my list, and I'm going to assume that whatever comes to my mind during this time of prayer is from You or is allowed by You. I'm going to let You lead my time of prayer."[13] If he got a tempting thought, he talked to God about that area of weakness. If it was a thought about how busy his day was, he discussed his plans with God. He actively engaged with God about whatever thoughts came to his mind, whether good, bad, or even tempting.

Before that night, his prayer life had primarily consisted of reading through lists he had made. He felt like he prayed in the flesh and rarely spent more than 8 minutes in prayer. That night, he had a conversation with God and spent 45 minutes feeling connected relationally. It was the first time he understood that praying in the Spirit is praying relationally with God.

---

12 | Neil T. Anderson, *Liberating Prayer* (Eugene: Harvest House, 2003, 2012) p. 19.
13 | *Liberating Prayer*, p. 24.

2) Prayer should always include gratitude. As Dr. Anderson read passages on living in the Spirit, he began to realize how often they urged gratitude, like Ephesians 5:18-20, "be filled with the Spirit . . . always giving thanks to God the Father for everything, in the name of our Lord Jesus Christ," and Colossians 3:15, "Let the peace of Christ rule in your hearts . . . And be thankful." Other Scriptures on the importance of gratitude began coming to mind, and he realized that praying in the Spirit requires an attitude of gratitude. This corresponds well with what Jim Wilder and his team wrote in *Joyful Journey*.

> Gratitude opens us up to the presence of God. Gratitude is a password into our awareness of God. We specifically chose gratitude because it is the easiest and fastest path to connection and because throughout Scripture God in His wisdom has always encouraged us to give thanks.[14]

Many godly people have discovered the importance of the practice of listening prayer. Here are just a few:

» John Eldredge, "The single most significant decision that has changed my prayer life more than any other, the one step that has brought about greater results than all the others combined is this (drum roll, please) . . . asking Jesus what I should pray."[15]

» A.W. Tozer, "Lord, teach me to listen. The times are noisy and my ears are weary with the thousand raucous sounds which continually assault them. . . . Let me hear Thee speaking in my heart. Let me get used to the sound of Thy Voice that its tones may be familiar when the sounds of earth die away and the only sound will be the music of Thy speaking Voice."[16]

---

14 | *Joyful Journey,* pp. 15-16.

15 | John Eldredge, *Moving Mountains: Praying with Passion, Confidence, and Authority* (Nashville: Thomas Nelson, 2016) p. 138.

16 | A.W. Tozer, *The Pursuit of God* (Chicago: Moody, 1948).

» Dallas Willard, "Learning to hear God is much more about becoming comfortable in a continuing conversation and learning to constantly lean on the goodness and love of God, than it is about turning God into an ATM for advice, or treating the Bible as a crystal ball." For Willard "learning the two-way communication between us and God" is a natural part of a kingdom life.[17]

As he began to develop this pattern of listening prayer, Dr. Anderson noticed something unexpected. Other thoughts came into his mind besides thoughts from God. He had thoughts like, "Don't forget to change the oil," or "Remember you have a meeting on Monday." Rather than fighting these thoughts, he simply wrote them down and got back to prayer. He also noticed another kind of distracting thought as he quieted himself to listen. He had thoughts like, "This is a waste of time," "You'll never be a real prayer warrior," and "who do you think you are?" Can you tell where these thoughts were coming from? He wrote these down in a separate spiral notebook. Paying attention to these negative, accusational thoughts helped him recognize the enemy's attack so he could take those thoughts captive.

IMMANUEL JOURNALING

One of the simplest and most transferable approaches to listening prayer we have found comes from the book *Joyful Journey* by Jim Wilder, John and Sungshing Loppnow, and Anna Kang. Their approach is based on the premise that God often shares "mutual mind" moments with us in which His thinking and ours get in sync. The goal of this process is to follow the brain's natural process for forming connections. In other words, it follows the joy elevator.

17 | Dallas Willard *Hearing God* (Downers Grove: InterVarsity Press, 1984, 2012). Quote from the Foreword to the 2012 expanded edition.

Step 1: <u>Interactive Gratitude</u>. It is common to encourage people to start their prayers with thankfulness and praise. Immanuel journaling takes this a step further and uses gratitude as the launching pad for conversation. Instead of simply writing out what we are grateful for, we stop and listen for spontaneous thoughts responding to our gratitude. Does Jesus have something to say about our appreciation? Writing those thoughts jumpstarts our time of conversational prayer.

Steps 2-6: <u>Texting with Jesus</u>. Once a connection has been established through interactive gratitude, the rest of the journaling time is done using first person ("I") as if Jesus is the one speaking. The point is not that we are taking dictation or that every word we write is from God. Rather, it is an opportunity to share a mutual mind moment with God and see where it takes our thoughts. This isn't meant to be an overwhelming journaling experience where you write an essay for each thought. Rather, you can think of it as texting with Jesus. Try following this outline, inspired by God's interaction with Moses in Exodus 3 and God's interaction with Hagar in Genesis 16 in which He saw someone with a problem, heard their cry for help (even if it was internal), and offered a solution.

» **I see you . . .** This can be as simple as "I see you typing on your laptop as you fly to Atlanta."

» **I hear you . . .** This is a reflection of what is really going on inside our hearts. If Jesus were listening to your heart, what would He hear? As I ask that question, I write, "I hear your concerns about the future. I hear you wondering if you have made mistakes so big there is no avoiding the consequences."

» **I know how big . . .** This part is about validation. Jesus not only hears us, He also knows how big the emotions are about what He hears. "I know how often you worry about the future and how many problems you face and how few solutions you have. I know how big that feels—like a weight you can never set down."

» **I am with you . . .** The next step is about connection. Jesus sees, hears, understands, and is happy to be present with us and go through life together. "I am with you and happy you are taking the time to bring this to Me. I don't want you to have to carry this on your own. Take My yoke—let Me share the burden."

» **I am strong . . .** The last step of the journaling process is an expression of God's ability to do something about what He sees, hears, understands, and joins us in handling. "I am strong enough to help. I have been down this road again and again. There is nothing coming up in your future I have not prepared for. The weight is more than you can handle, but it is an easy thing for Me. Trust Me, and let's do this together."

Step 7: <u>Share the Conversation</u>. The final step of Immanuel journaling is to read your journaling to someone else. There are a few good reasons for this.

1. Writing can be done just from the left side of your brain. Reading it to someone else activates the right hemisphere as well.

2. Sharing what you journal keeps you relationally connected.

3. Sharing what you write gives others a chance to check something that may be going in the wrong direction or affirm that something you have written sounds like what God would want you to know.

4. Reading to others helps move your writing from short term to long term memory.

Asking for word pictures

Many times in Scripture God didn't simply speak to people in words, He spoke in images. Jeremiah saw an almond branch and then God explained the meaning of the picture. Daniel saw visions that needed to be interpreted. Peter saw a vision of a sheet filled with unclean animals that led to his new understanding that Gentiles were welcome in God's family as well as Jews. The list of pictures and visions used by God to communicate is pretty extensive. For our purposes, the point is that God doesn't always speak to us with words. We need to learn to pay attention to images that come to mind as well.

I had an experience of this early in my marriage when an image of a beautiful teacup came to mind. I could tell by the context that the image represented how God wanted me to picture my wife. The picture of the teacup was followed by the words, "Be careful, Marcus, she is precious and fragile. Don't break her."

My friend Daryl Anderson has written a book of stories for husbands and wives to use to promote conversation.[18] Each of the stories in his book represents a word picture God gave him about a situation in his life. If you are looking for a collection of good samples of the listening prayer process, I recommend this book.

Sharing the journey with others

It is important to include others in the journey of practicing listening prayer. One reason for this is that learning to recognize God's voice is a skill and requires discernment. Having others listen to your journaling and give you feedback offers a form of protection. It can also be encouraging to others.

Let's face it, hearing from God is a skill that can be influenced both by the flesh and by demonic spirits. For example,

18 | Daryl A. Anderson, *Heart to Heart Connections: A Devotional Guide* (Colorado Springs: Lydia Press, 2006).

when I (Marcus) was in college, several guys told me they believed God wanted them to propose. In each case, they were totally serious. In each case, when they told me who it was, they named the same girl—who just happened to be, according to popular opinion, the prettiest girl in school. It wasn't too hard to see the influence of the flesh there.

Another friend told me he felt called to be a missionary in a country known at the time as the most dangerous place in the world to be a Christian. We talked for over an hour and pushed into this 'calling' a little deeper. Eventually, it came out that he felt God would love Him more if he signed up for the hardest job possible. That didn't seem like the Spirit. However, he did end up in ministry with the people group from that region, and I believe there was something of the Spirit in what he was sensing.

LEARNING TO RECOGNIZE GOD'S VOICE IS A SKILL AND REQUIRES DISCERNMENT.

I can go on and on with people who thought they heard from God about something, who either clearly didn't or heard something that was only partially on track. In fact, there have been times when I had to admit it would be simpler to rule out the idea of hearing God's voice altogether and just rely on trying to find a biblical principle for everything we face (which is how I used to live).

On the other hand, I have seen such profound healing occur through God's presence, have seen people find such peace and be led into such clear understanding of God and Scripture, that I know the Spirit was at work in those cases in some unmistakable ways. Rather than throw it all out, we need to learn discernment, and that requires feedback from a community.

To start, share your journaling about the "God thoughts" that come your way with someone you trust. Gradually build a team of at least three people you can share with. It has been interesting to me how often I have shared something from a time of journaling only to have it come alive in a new and more profound way as I shared it with someone else. I have also seen others impacted by something I had received even more deeply than it seemed to impact me.

In testing whether it is really God's voice you are hearing, we recommend two simple tests:

1. Does it lead to the fruit of the Spirit? Does the thought prompt you to greater love, joy, peace, patience, etc.? We would expect thoughts from the Spirit to lead to the fruit of the Spirit.

2. Does it contradict Scripture? If it does, then there is something clearly wrong.

At Deeper Walk, we encourage people to participate in Journey Groups. Whether online or in person, these groups are safe places to begin exploring listening prayer in a community setting. To learn more about how they work and where you can join one, visit DeeperWalkInternational.org.

A JOY WORKOUT

For today's joy workout we recommend that you practice Immanuel journaling as described on pp. 150-152.

Here is a guided prompt to get you started. Finish each phrase with two or three sentences that come to mind.

I am thankful for . . . .

Write the rest as if Jesus is speaking to you.
I see you . . .

I hear you asking . . .

I know how big this is . . .

I am happy to go through this with you . . .

I am strong enough to . . .

Share your journaling with someone you trust.

CONCLUSION

We hope this book has helped you understand how building bounce works and given you a clear path on how to grow your own emotional resilience.

We want to encourage you to make the ABCs of bounce a normal part of your life. Share the book with others who need encouragement and guidance, and find others you can partner with as you become intentional about growing your emotional capacity.

The purpose of this book has been to help you understand how emotional resilience works and to give you tools, strategies, and principles for growing your own emotional capacity and helping others build more bounce.

We have tried to keep the concepts simple and the work straightforward.

The goals:

1. Grow a bigger joy center.

2. Develop stronger pathways back to joy from upsetting emotions.

The strategies:

1. Appreciation – Practice five minutes each day, twice per day, for two months and watch what happens. Use the acrostic GAMES to help.

2. Beliefs – Read the Bible and meditate on it several times each week. Practice identifying and replacing the lies that drive negative emotions.

3. Connections – Practice the relational skills that help create belonging with people and go deeper in your walk with God through listening prayer.

We all get overwhelmed at times. But learning the ABCs of building bounce can transform the way you live. We pray you will find the tools and models presented in this book helpful in your own walk with God and in your ministry to others.

RESOURCES
go deeper

Throughout *Building Bounce* we've mentioned several books that could help you go deeper in these topics and on your walk with God. Here's a consolidated list plus bonus recommendations!

» *The 4 Habits of Joy-Filled Marriages*
Marcus Warner + Chris M. Coursey | Northfield Publishing

» *The Body Keeps the Score*
Bessel van der Kolk | Penguin Books

» *Captain Snout and the Super Power Questions*
Daniel Amen | Zonderkidz

» *The Complete Guide to Living With Men*
E. James Wilder | Shephard's House, Inc.

» *Could It Be This Simple?*
Timothy R. Jennings | Lennox Publishing

» *Daring Greatly*
Brené Brown | Gotham Books

» *Hearing God*
Dallas Willard | InterVarsity Press

» *Heart to Heart Connections*
Daryl Anderson | Lydia Discipleship Ministries

» *Joyful Journey*
E. James Wilder, et al. | Life Model Works

» *Liberating Prayer*
Neil T. Anderson | Harvest House

» *Living from the Heart Jesus Gave You*
E. James Wilder, Anne Bierling, et al. | Shephard's House, Inc.

» *Moving Mountains*
John Eldredge | Thomas Nelson

» *Outsmarting Yourself*
Karl Lehman | This Joy! Books

» *Passing the Peace*
E. James Wilder | Life Model Works

» *The Pursuit of God*
A. W. Tozer | Moody Publishers

» *Rare Leadership*
Warner + Wilder | Moody Publishers

» *REAL Prayer*
Marcus Warner | Deeper Walk

» *Secrets of the Vine*
Bruce Wilkinson | Multnomah

» *Six Hours One Friday*
Max Lucado | Multnomah

» *Slaying the Monster*
Marcus Warner | Deeper Walk

» *The Soul of Shame*
Curt Thompson | InterVarsity Press

» *Spiritual Warfare*
Karl Payne | WND Books

» *The Steps to Freedom in Christ*
Neil T. Anderson | Freedom in Christ Ministries

» *Strategic Business Prayer*
Dawn Whitestone | Deeper Walk

» *Taking Every Thought Captive*
Alaine Pakkala | Lydia Discipleship Ministries

» *Toward a Deeper Walk*
  Marcus Warner | Deeper Walk

» *Trauma Coping System*
  Melissa Finger | Seek First Ministries

» *Victory Over the Darkness*
  Neil T. Anderson | Bethany House

» *What Every Believer Should Know About Spiritual Warfare*
  Marcus Warner | Deeper Walk

appreciations

MARCUS

I am very grateful to Nik Harrang, Kim Jones, Dawn Whitestone and others who looked at this manuscript during its development. They combed this text and gave exceptional input that made this book much better than when it started.

It was a special delight to be able to work with my daughter Stephanie Warner, who served as the editor for this book (which is short for a one person publishing company). It was fun to sit at coffee shops together and be able to bond over this project.

Finally, I want to thank Stefanie Hinman for the inspiration to write this book and her generous spirit throughout the process.

STEFANIE

First, I would like to thank the ultimate Creator of all joy for His goodness! You are my secure base and source of life!

Thank you also to my family. To my amazing husband, John, and our four beautiful children, you remind me daily that life is beautiful and time is precious. You bring me much joy!

Thank you to Dr. Marcus Warner and Stephanie Warner for the time and energy they put into this project. I have learned much from you!

Finally, I would also like to thank the clients and families that have invited me into the most tender places of their stories. Knowing each of you has deeply impacted who I am and how I see the world. I have learned so much from you.

MARCUS WARNER

Marcus Warner (MDiv, ThM Old Testament, and DMin from Trinity Evangelical Divinity School) is the president of Deeper Walk International. He is a former pastor and college professor who has written several books on topics ranging from how to study the Bible to spiritual warfare, emotional healing, leadership, and marriage.

Marcus has done training events for organizations such as Navigators, Willow Creek Prison Ministry, and The Moody Church. He has traveled the world with Deeper Walk equipping people on the front lines of ministry with practical tools for dealing with root issues that keep people and ministries stuck and unable to go deeper into what God has for them.

STEFANIE HINMAN

Stefanie Hinman (Board-Certified Christian Counselor and Registered Art Therapist) is the founder of Healing Expressions, LLC where she works with individuals, families, schools, and organizations in the areas of trauma healing and recovery, crisis intervention, and building resilient kids, families, and communities.

Stefanie has worked with families and children for over 20 years as they journey through life's more difficult seasons. Adversity is a part of the human experience, joy is the key to navigating it well. Stefanie's passion is to help others build joy and emotional resilience so that when adversity comes, they will have the capacity to bounce back. Connect with her at www.healingexpressionskc.com.

Deeper Walk International is a 501(C)(3) nonprofit bringing together biblically-balanced teaching on emotional healing and spiritual warfare that helps people who feel stuck break through to new levels of freedom in their walk with God.

We teach about God's grace, life in the Spirit, spiritual warfare, and authentic community. What sets our training apart is how we bring it all together, then make it simple and transferable, so that people understand what it takes to walk in freedom and grow in maturity.

We call this approach to ministry "heart-focused discipleship."

Find us at DeeperWalkInternational.org.

the world wounds us

the devil lies to us

we vow never to let it happen again

we spend our lives picking the fruit of our wounds

It doesn't have to stay this way.

Flesh-filled homes breed conflict and pain.

Spirit-filled homes grow the maturity to
handle hard things in loving ways.

These and other resources can be found at
www.DeeperWalkInternational.org

Made in the USA
Monee, IL
04 June 2021